THE HOMEOWNER'S SURVIVAL KIT

THE HOMEOWNER'S SURVIVAL KIT

How to Beat the High Cost of Owning and Operating Your Home

by A. M. Watkins

HAWTHORN BOOKS, INC. *Publishers*
NEW YORK

THE HOMEOWNER'S SURVIVAL KIT

2   3   4   5   6   7   8   9   10

CONTENTS

LIST OF
ILLUSTRATIONS

FOREWORD

ENERGY SHORTAGES have burst upon us in the United States since the first edition of this book, "The Home-Owner's Survival Kit," was written and published just a few years ago. For the first time in our history as a nation, barring wartime, we are no longer brimming over with an abundance of all the energy and other supplies of life that we formerly took for granted—and often used up with thriftless abandon.

Shortages bring forth with them rising costs. Government studies indicate that, because of shortages, the cost of household energy—gas, electricity and fuel oil—will rise by 5 to 10 percent a year in the next decade and a half. With household gas, for which the steepest price rises are likely, that could mean a doubling in your home heating and other gas costs in the next decade, and a four-fold increase in your same bills within the next fifteeen years or so. No bright future to look forward to there.

You can, however, keep down your gas and other energy bills considerably in the future, also do much to keep down other monthly, housing expenses like telephone and repair bills, and we tell you how in the following pages. Here in this book is a plethora of money-saving facts and practical information designed to help you cope with the seemingly endless problems and expense encountered with running a house and household nowadays. Much of the material can help you considerably should you rent a house or apartment, as well as when you own a house.

This book can be a great helpmate and money saver for you because housing now accounts for the biggest single expense in the typical American family's annual living costs. Housing accounts for some 30 percent of the typical American family's living costs, by far the number one expenditure. Food was formerly first but is now second, accounting for some 25 percent of the average family's expenditure.

The heaviest burden generally falls on the home-owning family with growing children and growing housing expenses. Inflation in recent years has made it worse, especially with housing costs rising faster, and more painfully, than almost any other individual living cost.

It is clearly getting tougher and more expensive to survive. But this book can help you fight back successfully. It not only contains much practical information on how to beat the high cost of owning and operating a house, but also on how to win over continual vicissitudes encountered almost daily in our houses and homes where we spend up to two-thirds of our lives. Here is a sampling of the specific subjects dealt with:

- How to save 20 to 30 percent on your home heating bills.
- Why your annual property taxes may be 10 percent too high and what to do about it.
- Twenty-one ways to save energy and save on your gas and electric bills.
- How to avoid home repair bills.
- Three key ways to reduce summer cooling bills.
- Save up to 25 percent on your home insurance cost, often get an immediate refund.
- The most expensive income-tax trap to avoid when you own a house.
- Four common mistakes that make your house a target for thieves and how to correct them.
- A broker's trade secrets for selling a house at the highest price.
- Plus many ways to save when you rent as well as own.

To help you make important economies, various cost figures are cited throughout this book; most were in effect at the time this book went to press. Because of inflation, however, you must make allowances for subsequent price increases that will inevitably occur between the time this book went to press and when you may read it. Although some of the prices cited may no longer be accurate, the underlying facts about each subject, such as how to save on your telephone bills, utility costs, and so on, should nonetheless still be accurate and valid.

Your house and home should not be a continuing burden and bore. It should be instead, a continuing source of pleasure. By knowing how to master and control the various costs and responsibilities that go with owning a house, more time, money and attention can be devoted to obtaining pleasure from other pursuits in life. Helping you to achieve that objective is probably the most important goal of this book.

A. M. WATKINS

CHAPTER 1 HOW TO SAVE ON YOUR
ANNUAL PROPERTY TAXES AND
MORTGAGE PAYMENTS

*Are you paying too much in property taxes? How to tell and
what to do about it if you are . . . Special tax assessments . . .
Qualifying for a tax exemption . . . Reducing your household-
property tax . . . Tax-deductible savings on your income tax . . .
Saving on mortgage interest payments . . . What you must do
now to get the maximum tax benefits on one of the biggest
single taxes ever paid by homeowners (when you sell a house
at a profit).*

THE REAL-ESTATE property tax is usually the biggest single expense
associated with owning a house. It's what you pay for your share
of the construction cost and upkeep of local streets, sewers, and
schools and for the operation of local government. Most communities rely on the property tax for 80 to 90 per cent of their total
annual municipal budget.

As a result, and as many homeowners painfully know, property
taxes have climbed to record levels in recent years. They have,
in fact, climbed at two to three times the average rate of increase
in the cost of living in the last decade. Property taxes run up to
fifteen hundred dollars to two thousand dollars a year now on
many suburban houses for which they were formerly no more than
five hundred dollars to six hundred dollars. Property taxes and the
monthly mortgage payment, which are often combined into one
monthly payment, now account for the largest single annual
living expense for many families.

There are ways, however, to soften the blow of your property-

1

tax and mortgage bill. Both, for example, are tax-deductible items on your federal income-tax return and also on the income tax paid in nearly all of the more than forty states with state income taxes. Not everybody, though, gets the full benefit of the tax-deductible savings that can result.

Another potential tax, often coming out of the blue when you've owned a house, can hit you harder than any other single one-time tax you will pay in your lifetime. That's the tax you must pay on your profit when you sell a house. This tax is only deferred—not canceled, as some people believe—when you sell a house and shortly afterward buy another house. The shock of this tax can be substantially cushioned, however, if you know about it in advance.

Let's talk first about property taxes and what can sometimes be done to reduce them. Property taxes are not always fair, accurate, or equitably levied. The property tax on your house may be unfairly high because, of all things, the local assessor made a simple mistake. He may have incorrect information about your house. One expert assessor says, "We sometimes find houses that actually cost as little as half of what our records say." That, of course, can make your tax bill twice what it should be (until you have it corrected). Overall, a 10 per cent error on local property taxes is quite common, another assessor says. In fact, he adds that being that close to absolute value is "considered good."

ARE YOU PAYING TOO MUCH IN PROPERTY TAXES?

Here's how to tell and what to do about it if you are. Fundamentally, your property tax is based on the assessed valuation of your house. How this works and a common misunderstanding that results are illustrated by the case of Jack and Bonnie Todd (not their real names). Their house was assessed for $6,100, which did not bother them because it was worth about $30,000. Nor were they bothered that the assessments on a few neighbors' houses much like their house were somewhat lower than theirs. They paid a few dollars more in taxes, they figured, but not enough to fuss about.

The Todds hit the ceiling when they discovered that they paid about 20 per cent more in property taxes than their neighbors paid. The assessment on one neighbor's house was just under $5,000, and two others were at $5,000. The Todds' $6,100 assessment being some 20 per cent higher was, of course, the reason they paid more. They took their case to the local tax assessor and demonstrated that their house was worth no more than the other, similar houses nearby that had lower assessments. As a result their assessment was lowered, and their taxes came down nearly 20 per cent.

The Todds learned two important things about property taxes. The dollar figure of your assessment may be comparatively close to those of similar houses, but this can be misleading. It is the percentage defference that counts. Secondly, your house may be assessed at a comparatively low figure compared with what your house is worth (its current market value), but nevertheless your annual tax bill may be excessively high.

Your tax bill, by the way, is determined by applying the local tax rate to the assessed valuation of your house. There's little you can do about the tax rate. It's the same for everyone where you live. The tax rate also can vary from year to year, up or down (though lately it seems only to go upward). Sometimes you will get one overall tax bill a year for your share of all village, town, county, and local school taxes. It may come to, say, $10 per $100 of assessed property value. A house assessed at $7,000 is therefore taxed a total of $700 for the year ($10 times 70). It may be based on the "mill," a thousandth of a dollar. A 90-mill rate on a $7,000 assessment gives a tax bill of $630 ($0.09 times 7,000).

Sometimes the tax is broken down, and separate bills are sent to you by the local village or city, and also by the town, county, and state. Each bills you for the tax due it. The local school district may also send its bill for your share of school

The local property taxes on these four houses, located in four different parts of the country, vary from under $600 to $2,500 a year, though there is much less difference in the market value and construction cost of each house. The large variation in taxes stems from the value of the land under each house and the local property-tax rate.

expenses directly to you. Each will use a uniform tax rate based on dollars per $100 of assessed value. Your city tax may run, say, $4.07 per $100, state and county, $3.47 per $100; and the local school tax rate, often the highest, $7.65 per $100. Adding all of those up gives a total tax rate of $15.19 per $10 of assessed valuation.

CHECKING YOUR ASSESSMENT

This is the first thing to do in determining whether or not your annual tax bill is unfairly high. If it is, you then appeal for a reduced assessment.

Your house-assessment figure should be noted on a recent tax bill, or you could call the tax assessor's office for it. Let's say your house is assessed at $7,500, though it is worth $30,000 today. That means that your assessment is *apparently* based on a 25 per cent ratio of assessment to actual market value ($7,500 being 25 per cent of $30,000). The ratio used will vary from community to community, ranging from as little as 5 or 10 per cent of actual market value up to 100 per cent. In most communities, however, the ratio runs from about 20 to 50 per cent. (Fortunately, there is a trend toward higher ratios. That's good, because the higher the assessment ratio, the less the likelihood of local tax inequities. Conversely, if a low ratio is used locally, there's a greater likelihood that your house may be unfairly assessed.) If a 30 per cent ratio is used locally, a house worth $30,000 would be assessed at $9,000 (.30 times $30,000), a $40,000 house would be assessed at $12,000 (.30 times $40,000), and so on.

Remember, however, that the market value of your house which is used to determine your assessment is not necessarily what your house is worth now or what it was worth in the very recent past. It may be what your house was worth up to ten or more years ago, the year in which the last general assessment was made. It may have been five years ago, and housing costs have since risen by, say, 20 per cent. All properties nonetheless

The property taxes on most houses in this community are approximately equal. They're based largely on the sales prices of the houses, which were built a few years ago. The taxes, however, are by and large higher than those for older houses with comparable market value located nearby.

continue to be assessed according to their value five years ago. A house that is worth $30,000 today would therefore be valued for assessment purposes at $25,000, its presumed value five years ago.

Take that into account when you check your assessment. A clerk in the local tax office can tell you exactly how assessments are figured locally. He should also tell you exactly how your assessment was figured. Don't be shy, by the way, about calling at the tax office and asking. Nobody will bite you, and inquiring about your house taxes does not automatically bring down on you the wrath of the tax assessor. People come by every day for one reason or another, and answering their questions is routine for most assessors and their assistants. There are exceptions, of course; a few assessors are political hacks or angry, vindictive men, treating nearly every inquiry about your tax as a personal affront (unless you happen to be locally prominent). Fortunately, such assessors are in a minority.

THE COMPARISON TEST

Next, compare your assessment with those of neighbors' houses of similar size and value. This is the acid test for determining whether or not your assessment is fair and equitable. It should be in line with the assessments on nearby houses. If it is not, something could be wrong, as the Todds found out.

The assessments on all other houses and other property in an area should be listed in the assessment book at your tax office. As a rule, anyone can walk in and see this book; real-estate people do it all the time. By law the book, usually located in the lobby of the tax office, must be open to the public. From it you can make a list of nearby houses with their assessed valuations. Often this can quickly indicate whether or not your assessment is out of line.

When you compare assessments, keep in mind that older houses tend to be assessed lower than new houses—sometimes incredibly lower. It's partly because depreciation takes its toll of an older house, partly because the actual present-day value of an older house is harder to determine than that of a new house (which recently sold at a known price), and also because some tax assessors tend to favor older residents over those who moved in recently. This last should not be so, especially when outrageously low assessments result. On the other hand, such low assessments might help you get a better deal on your house. That's if you show that your house is decidedly over-assessed in relation to comparable houses nearby with low assessments.

Now you should have a good idea of how your assessment was figured and whether or not it is accurate and fair. Let's say you've visited the assessor's office and politely inquired about your house. The clerk pulled out your card and explained how your house is assessed. Here, by the way, you should check on the price written down as what you paid for your house. If this figure is wrong, it should be easily correctible, and you're off and running. Are the other figures right? What about the value put on your lot as opposed to the value on the house structure by itself? The lot (your land) is usually figured separately and then added to the value of your house to give the total property value.

APPEALING YOUR ASSESSMENT

If you believe your house is over-assessed, you generally follow a specific procedure to get it reduced. The procedure will vary from town to town, so find out about this in your area when you talk to the assessor. In most areas you present your appeal for a reduced assessment on a special day each year, such as "Grievance Day." When you do, be civil, polite, and let your facts speak for themselves. Keep your cool. This is an important point to remember.

You may also have to state your case to a board of review, sometimes called the board of relief. You're entitled to a private hearing, if desired, and you may, if you wish, bring along a lawyer. Special rules and regulations may have to be met, depending on state and local laws and customs.

It can help to put your appeal in writing, at least for your own use, if you make a verbal presentation. Muster your facts effectively. You might consult a local lawyer for guidance, merely paying him a consultation fee based on the hour or so of his time you require. You could also hire a lawyer to handle your appeal completely, and then his fee will, of course, be more. Sometimes it's a fixed fee, arranged with you in advance; other times it's based on at least one half of the total taxes saved the first year if he wins the appeal.

Basically, an appeal for a lower assessment is a presentation that shows why your house is actually worth less than the assessor values it for tax purposes. Your house may be worth, for example, $32,000, but the assessor has it down for $42,000. To prove your case you generally must get written appraisals from two or three professional real-estate appraisers who substantiate the lower appraisal value of your house. This by itself should clearly demonstrate that the assessor's figure is too high. If you can back this up with facts showing that comparable houses nearby are assessed according to the lower figure, that's all to the good.

You might also show that the present condition of your house makes it worth less than the assessor says. Facts about the structure and neighborhood come into play here. For example, a house with wood-frame walls is usually valued less than one of brick or stone. Steel or iron plumbing usually rates a deduction of up to 10 per cent compared with the value put on modern copper plumbing. Plasterboard walls are valued lower than plaster, and in some areas warm-air heat is valued less than hot-water or steam heat. Allowances also should be made for structural depreciation. Your house may have an old-fashioned kitchen or bathroom or a run-down structural condition. This reduces its value in the market place and therefore should lower its assessed value too.

Just as a splendid river view will make your house highly desirable and more valuable to a potential buyer, thus causing a higher assessment, undesirable neighborhood characteristics will, on the other hand, downgrade its value. A noisy new highway, jet airport, or new commercial development nearby can depreciate the value of a house and therefore justify a reduced assessment.

If your appeal for a reduced assessment is turned down, you can take your case to court, although doing this is not necessarily advisable. If you believe you have an excellent case and the potential tax savings are large, by all means consider a court appeal. The legal expense, however, may be higher than what you would save on taxes. Even if you win, the court ruling may stand for only a year or so. After that you could be hit again with another high assessment by a vindictive Board of Assessors. In most cases, though, you will get a fair hearing. If you are over-assessed, a well-documented appeal together with an effective presentation will result in a new, lower assessment and a lower annual tax bill.

A FEW FACTS ABOUT PROPERTY TAXES IN GENERAL

In many areas the property tax is administered and levied in a sloppy, if not appallingly shocking, manner. Very low assessment-to-actual-value ratios are used, which often perpetuate ridiculously low taxes for a favored few. Everybody else pays more to make up the difference. Politics often enters the picture, with the party in power favoring its members with unfairly low assessments and hitting members of the other party with excessively stiff ones. There is much room for national reform, though a growing number of communities are instituting long-overdue improvements in assessment practices.

Many assessments, for example, are the result of what was formerly a "horseback" appraisal. An assessor on horseback would ride by, and pausing but not dismounting, would jot down the value of a house based on a fast glance or two. Today it's done too frequently by "windshield" or "curbstone" appraisal. Your house is given a fast look by an assessor who never leaves his car. If your house was appraised that way, you could well have a justifiable request for a reassessment.

There are, in brief, "gross inequities," as stated about the real-estate property-tax situation in the United States in a report by the Advisory Commission on Intergovernmental Relations, a national nonprofit group especially concerned with civic matters. Singlehandedly, you may be unable to make any earth-shaking reforms in the national problem, but if an arbitrary, old-fashioned property-tax situation exists where you live, here are a few suggestions on what can be done about it. Every community, city, and town should have a trained, full-time professional assessor who is beyond the oily reach of politics. The old idea of a small part-time assessment board should not be tolerated. Getting a full-time professional assessor, however, often requires steady pressure from property owners, civic clubs, and women's organizations. More and more towns also hire an expert independent appraisal firm to reappraise periodically all the property within their limits. Such companies, by and large, are honest and highly capable, but a few have been known to be influenced by local politicians. To prevent this, a nonpartisan citizens' committee should investigate the firms being considered for your general reassessment. . . .

Now back to your house taxes and other ways to reduce them.

DO YOU QUALIFY FOR A TAX EXEMPTION?

Exemptions are often given to war veterans, people over sixty-five, widows, and sometimes the blind. There are also homestead exemptions given in certain states (Alabama, Arkansas, California, Florida, Georgia, Iowa, Louisiana, Missouri, Mississippi, Oklahoma, South Dakota, Texas, West Virginia, and Wyoming).

In effect, an exemption gives you a discount on your tax. In some cases it can be quite large, reducing your tax bill by as much as 50 to 100 per cent. Because the exemptions vary from city to city and state to state, you must ask your tax assessor about possible exemptions given locally and who qualifies for them.

The amount of your exemption also can increase from time to time. Even if you benefit from an exemption obtained in the past, you may rate a larger one now. In some states, for example, veterans' benefits received each year from the government, including, of all things, G.I.-insurance dividends, can boost your property-tax exemption. Look into this, too.

Incidentally, property-tax exemptions also have led to many flagrant abuses and should be abolished, some experts say. Other types of aid should be given to the deserving. For example, giving property-tax exemptions to war veterans may sound worthy, but it doesn't always work. In New York State, for example, the veterans'-exemption law is so written that a veteran with long and distinguished service may get very little benefit, while another with little service gets a very large tax reduction every year.

PROPERTY-TAX TIPS

Pay your property taxes on time, and you'll avoid the usual penalty for late payment. Sometimes you can save money if you pay in advance. In one state, for example, real-estate taxes are due in March. Pay just before March 1, and you earn a 3½ per cent discount; pay after April 1, and you're hit with a 9 per cent penalty charge. Planning ahead for your tax bills could save you a stiff late-payment penalty. Pay ahead, and you may save more money on the discount earned than the same money would earn in interest if you had kept it in the bank.

HOUSEHOLD PROPERTY

In more than thirty states your household property—appliances, furniture, rugs, pictures, etc.—is also subject to a property tax. If the real-estate property tax inhabits a chaotic thicket of varying rules and standards, the household- or personal-property tax is a veritable no-man's-land.

More than half of the states with this tax allow a fixed deduction, which can range from one hundred dollars per taxpayer in some states up to five thousand dollars in others. A few states also give your local government the option to exempt all household property, but even with no official local option, in most places the tax is subject to local custom. (In many cases it's really a tax on integrity, a national task force of distinguished experts said. As a result, it's a sham. The honest taxpayer, honestly declaring his possessions, is penalized. With others, "The ease with which the law is evaded has created for it a notorious disrespect," the committee reported.)

Before you declare the value of your household property, consult experienced people in your area to find out the local customs.

It may be customary, for example, to list a TV set at twenty-five dollars no matter what its size, condition, or real value. Or you may be allowed to figure the total value of your household property as a percentage of your rent or of the assessed valuation of your house. Inquire about such things before you declare.

Automobiles are also covered by the household tax in more than twenty states, which calls for you to determine the customary procedure for declaring its value where you live. If you plan to buy a new car, you might delay the purchase until after the formal day of assessment for the year. Then you will not be taxed on it till next year and then only on its used-car value.

INCOME-TAX SAVINGS

These can bring about sizable annual savings when you own a house. The savings come in the form of reduced annual income taxes. It's because nearly all property taxes paid on a house are tax deductible on your federal income-tax return. So is the interest (but not the principal) paid each year on your house mortgage. Both are also tax deductible in most, if not all, of the more than forty states with state income taxes.

To benefit, you must itemize these and other deductions you are entitled to. Use the standard deduction, the so-called short-method return, and you will usually pay a higher income tax if you own a house. Tax experts estimate that hundreds of thousands, and possibly several million, homeowners pay more income tax than necessary, and thus lose money, by taking the standard deduction—also called the give-up method. This denies you the tax-deductible benefits of property taxes and mortgage-interest payments. If in doubt about which method to use, figure your income tax both ways, with and without the standard deduction. Then use the one that gives the smaller tax. This is a perfectly honest and legitimate procedure, and among other things, it's recommended by Internal Revenue Service officials.

MORTGAGE PAYMENTS

Never underestimate the deductible benefits of a house-mortgage loan. Among other things, this can mean that you should not pay off your mortgage as soon as possible, or you will lose money. That's compared with retaining your mortgage and paying no more than necessary for it until its very end.

Consider, for example, that the cost of a 6 per cent mortgage to a person in the 30 per cent tax bracket is actually 4 per cent, since 30 per cent of his interest charge is deducted from his federal income tax. Similarly, the same person "pays" only 4.9 per cent for a 7 per cent mortgage and 5.6 per cent net cost for an 8 per cent mortgage. His net mortgage cost is even lower if he also pays a state income tax, because of the additional savings on this tax. Exactly what your mortgage costs you depends, of course, on your mortgage interest rate and your tax bracket.

Should you pay off your mortgage as soon as possible or whittle it down, off and on, whenever you have extra cash for an extra payment? Paying off the mortgage does not make financial sense if the same money might earn more for you if it were kept in the bank, in blue-chip stocks or bonds, or invested safely anywhere else where the dividend return is equal to or higher than the net cost of your mortgage. Besides, keeping your money in a liquid investment means you'll have access to it in an emergency.

In addition, if you pay off your mortgage or just whittle it down faster than necessary, you may be subject to a prepayment charge which is often made when a mortgage is paid up ahead of time. You may find it tougher to sell your house in the future. If you have a large mortgage, a buyer can sometimes take it over with a relatively small cash down-payment. A small mortgage or none at all will require either new financing or a large down-payment that the buyer cannot manage, and this could mean the loss of the sale.

Finally, paying off your mortgage could lose you the tax-deductible income-tax benefits of your property taxes and other deductible expenses. That would happen if your total tax-deductible expenses, no longer including your mortgage interest, fall below the level of the standard deduction offered you on the income-tax form. That could hurt.

The case for and against paying off your mortgage obviously depends on how the economics work out for you. Figure your net cost and savings both ways—what you will gain by paying it off versus the income-tax savings and other gains if you invested the same money in another way.

Usually the main argument in favor of paying off a mortgage is the emotional relief that this act brings to some people. They feel relieved as a result of paying off a major debt and owning their houses free and clear. If this is important to you, by all means let your feelings be heard. Do, however, figure the possible cost and savings with and without a mortgage, and then your feelings may change—or be confirmed; if your mortgage interest is at a really high rate, paying it off as soon as possible could well be economically sensible (unless you can refinance your house at a reduced interest rate).

OTHER INCOME-TAX SAVINGS

Three other areas associated with owning a house (and sometimes with renting a house or apartment) can offer savings on your income tax: using a room or two of your house for business, which is often overdone (and followed by a call from the Internal Revenue Service); sustaining a casualty loss, which is often overlooked; and paying a special tax assessment, which is often misinterpreted.

If, for example, one of eight rooms of your house is used as a business office, one eighth of your total housing expenses then can be claimed as a deductible business expense on your income-tax returns. You must, however, be able to prove that the space is definitely used for business, and you must keep records of all your housing expenses, including a cleaning woman, as well as heat, light, insurance, taxes, and everything else.

A casualty loss is the damage sustained by your house or property from such things as fire, storm, flood, vandalism, or theft. Again, you must be able to prove the extent of the loss. Naturally, an insurance payment received for the loss will reduce the amount of the loss claimed as a deductible.

A special assessment for a new sewer system, water line, street, or any other such public improvement is tax deductible only if the improvement does not add to the value of your house. New sidewalks, streets, or a new sewer system will generally increase the value of your house. The special tax assessment you pay for such improvements is not tax deductible on your income-tax return. If the improvement does not increase the value of your property, it is deductible. A special tax for the local library, for example, generally will not affect the value of your house and is therefore deductible.

Determining the exact income-tax rule that applies to each of these housing items, as well as to all others mentioned in this chapter, can get intricate and involved. They also may be changed from one year to another. As a result, if you believe you may claim a tax deduction for one or more of them, check the latest I.R.S. rules to find out which apply. Get a copy of *Your Federal Income Tax*, one of the best tax-guide booklets, which sells for less than a dollar at any Internal Revenue Service office. Or, of course, discuss the matter with your income-tax accountant.

SELLING A HOUSE AT A PROFIT

This brings up one of the least understood taxes on houses, though it can be the largest of all taxes associated with home ownership. It's the tax due on the profit made when you sell a house. That, of course, is the difference between the cost of the house to you and the sales price when you sell it for more than your cost. If your house cost twenty thousand dollars, for example, and you sell it ten years later for thirty thousand dollars, you have a ten-thousand-dollar profit, and it is subject to a capital-gains tax. You may buy another house for thirty thousand dollars or more within twelve months or build another house within eighteen months, and then this tax is deferred. It is not canceled, as many people mistakenly believe.

The tax may be continually deferred if you buy and sell a series of houses over many years, but ultimately it must be paid, based on the accumulated profits going back, if necessary, to the very first house you bought. The tax is due when you sell a house at a profit and do not use all the sales money received to buy another house within a year or build a new house within eighteen months. The profit made on other houses you previously owned and sold is then also subject to the tax.

Your ultimate tax bill can be kept down, however—often substantially—if you have records of all the money you spent to buy, own, and sell each house, such as closing costs, brokers' fees, and money spent to remodel and improve a house while you lived in it. In other words, the basic cost of the house is the price you paid to buy it plus certain purchase expenses plus the cost of all capital improvements (but not ordinary maintenance and repairs) plus certain sales expenses. The cost of a new room, new kitchen or bath, or of any other such improvement increases the basic cost of the house. As a result, it reduces the profit when you later sell the house.

You will need bills, receipts, check stubs, or other records to substantiate such expenses, so keep all such records going back to the initial purchase of the very first house you bought. Not every expenditure made for a house may be a legitimate deduction for this tax. Paying a repairman to fix a roof leak or service the furnace or a painter to paint the house is ordinary maintenance and not deductible. An exception is money spent on final repairs in order to sell the house, such as the cost of painting,

A handsome new house like this one in a small Midwestern town is virtually certain to grow in value through the years. It is important to keep financial records for a house, starting from the time it is bought; this can mean a reduced tax on the profit when the house is sold.

sidewalk-patching, and other work of this nature. That's part of the sales cost, and so is the commission paid to a real-estate broker to sell the house; both are tax deductible. If in doubt, keep records of every dollar spent on your house. Later you can determine which are legitimate deductions.

Suppose you have already bought and sold a house at a profit and shortly afterward bought another house at a higher price, which deferred your tax on the profit from the first house. Remember that sometime in the future you will have to pay a tax on that profit. Even if a homeowner, at the end of a long life, dies before he pays the tax, it still must be paid, plucked in whole from a spouse, an heir, or his estate. This and the other many ins and outs of the tax due when you sell a house are explained in a government pamphlet, *Tax Information on Selling Your Home*. It's available free from any office of the Internal Revenue Service or from the Internal Revenue Service, Washington, D.C. 20224.

SELLING A HOUSE AT A LOSS

Unfortunately, the loss sustained on a house sale is ordinarily not tax deductible. And the loss cannot be subtracted from the profit made on another house you owned and sold prior to the one you sold at a loss.

The loss is tax deductible only if the house sold was a business investment. Therefore, if you anticipate that you must sell your house at a loss, possibly taking it on the chin with a large loss, you might consider renting the house instead of selling it. Rent it in good faith for at least six months and later sell it at a loss, and the loss can be deducted on your income-tax return. It is treated as a loss from the sale of business property!

While you rent the house, you could also benefit from other real-estate-tax benefits such as a depreciation deduction. The rules here can get complicated, and it's therefore advisable to discuss the tax intricacies with a good tax accountant or lawyer. Do this before you rent your house with the expectation of obtaining a future business loss.

SPECIAL TAX BENEFITS FOR PEOPLE SIXTY-FIVE AND OVER

If you are sixty-five years old or over, part or all of the tax on the profit from the sale of a house may be canceled. It's canceled if the house is sold at a net price of $20,000 or less. Say your house cost you $16,000 (its original price to you plus purchase expenses, capital improvements, etc.) and you sell it for a net price of $19,500, or $3,500 profit. If you are sixty-five or over, you are exempt from the tax on that profit.

If you sell the house for more than $20,000, a portion of the profit is tax-free. The tax-free portion is the ratio of $20,000 to the net sales price of the house multiplied by the total profit. It's not a simple formula, so here's an example. Suppose a house that cost you $16,000 is later sold for $25,500. You had $1,500 of sales expenses (real-estate broker's sales commission, other expenses to sell the house). That means a net sales price of $24,000 ($25,500 minus $1,500). Your profit on the house was $8,000 ($24,000 minus $16,000).

If you are sixty-five or older, the tax-free portion of the profit is $20,000/$24,000 times $8,000, or $6,667. You pay a tax only on the balance ($1,333).

To qualify for this tax exemption, you must have lived in the house for at least five of the eight years preceding the sale. If the house was jointly owned by a man and his wife, at least one must have been sixty-five at the time of the sale, and the husband and wife must file a joint federal income-tax return for the year during which the house was sold.

We emphasize again that this and other tax-law requirements may be modified or changed in the future as changes and different interpretations are made in our income-tax laws. As a result, information in this chapter and elsewhere in this book may no longer apply because of a new development or government ruling occurring after this book has gone to press; also, the government and the courts are continually changing their interpretation of our tax laws. To be sure about a particular aspect of taxes which may apply to your house, it's recommended that you check the latest provisions of the income-tax laws.

CHAPTER 2 UTILITIES: REDUCING
YOUR MONTHLY BILLS FOR ELECTRICITY,
GAS, AND WATER

■ *The most important causes of high monthly utility bills and*
what to do about them ... How to determine whether gas or
electricity is cheaper for your house ... Choosing appliances
and equipment for low operating cost ... Twenty-one cost-saving
tips ... Lighting and light bulbs ... How to check your
monthly bills ... Reducing water bills.

LIKE HOUSE taxes, bills for electricity, gas, and often water, too,
come due with inexorable regularity and must be paid (unless,
of course, you have your own Little Giant generating plant).
Sometimes they may seem unduly high, but trying to make sense
out of a utility bill seems hopeless. They're paid ruefully, perhaps, or with an occasional snarl and a few unkind words directed
at the local utility.

Actually, something can often be done about high monthly
household-utility bills. Many families are loaded down with as
many as forty or fifty different power-consuming household appliances—count your own, if this figure sounds exaggerated. The
result is an annual bill of three hundred dollars to five hundred
dollars a year for the fuel and energy to keep such equipment
going, as well as that needed to light your house. That doesn't
count the cost of house-heating and air conditioning, each of
which can have a whopping appetite for energy by itself. (Both
are dealt with in separate chapters later.)

The total bill each month for regular household utilities often
can be reduced, sometimes considerably so. To do this requires,
first of all, an understanding of where your utility dollars go
each month. The amount of power used by various household appliances is shown in the tables on pages 24–25 and 26.

Electricity Used by Typical Appliances

Electrical Appliance	Average Power Required, Watts	Average Total Power in Kw. Hrs. Consumed Annually
Airconditioner, room	1,485	750–1,500**
Air conditioning, 3-ton central*	4,500	3,000–6,000**
Blanket, electric	180	145
Broiler	1,430	110
Clock	2	17
Clothes dryer*	4,695	965
Coffee maker	910	100
Deep-fat fryer	1,420	85
Dehumidifier	265	350
Dishwasher	1,200	360
Egg cooker	510	14
Fan, attic	370	285
Fan, circulating	90	45
Fan, furnace	280	400
Fan, roll-about	185	130
Fan, window	190	165
Floor polisher	315	15
Food blender	345	14
Food freezer, 15 cu. ft.	335	1,120
Food freezer, frostless, 15 cu. ft.	425	1,685
Food mixer	125	12
Food-waste disposer*	420	25
Frying pan	1,180	190
Germicidal lamp	20	145
Grill, sandwich	1,150	35
Hair dryer	325	11
Heat lamp, infrared	250	14
Heat pump*	12,075	15,750**
Heater, radiant*	1,320	175
Heating pad	60	9

The table can tell you the approximate operating cost of nearly fifty electric appliances in houses. The figures are from a national survey by the Edison Electric Institute, the electric companies' trade association. They are average figures for typical use of each appliance.

The first column gives the power drawn by each appliance when it is turned on. It's the same standard unit of electric power, the watt, used for electric light bulbs, electric motors, and other electric devices. A heating pad, for example, draws 60 watts of power and therefore uses the same quantity of electricity as a 60-watt bulb.

The second column is more indicative of operating cost. It gives the total average electricity commonly used by each device in a year. Divide any figure in this column by 12 to get average monthly power consumption. Thus a dishwasher will use about 30 kilowatt hours of electricity a month.

A kilowatt hour is a function of the watt input to a device and the

Electrical Appliance	Average Power Required, Watts	Average Total Power in Kw. Hrs. Consumed Annually
Hot plate*	1,260	90
Humidifier	115	150
Iron, hand	1,085	150
Iron, mangle	1,465	165
Knife, carving	90	3
Oil burner or stoker*	260	410
Radio	80	90
Radio-phonograph	115	110
Range*	12,140	1,160
Refrigerator, 12 cu. ft.	240	675
Refrigerator, frostless, 12 cu. ft.	310	1,040
Refrigerator-freezer, 14 cu. ft.	330	1,085
Refrigerator-freezer, frostless, 14 cu. ft.	435	1,660
Roaster	1,330	215
Sewing machine	75	11
Shaver	14	3
Sun lamp	280	16
Television, black-and-white	250	345
Television, color	330	450
Toaster	1,140	40
Tooth brush	9	5
Vacuum cleaner	600	45
Vibrator	40	2
Waffle iron	1,095	20
Washing machine, automatic	515	105
Washing machine, non-automatic	285	80
Water heater, standard*	2,430	4,170
Water heater, quick recovery*	4,475	4,600
Water pump	435	225

* Also available in gas-operated models.
** Depends on local climate.

length of time it is used. For example, a 100-watt device operated for 10 hours will consume 1,000 watt hours, or 1 kilowatt hour, of electricity (100 times 10); a 500-watt device operated for 10 hours consumes 5,000 watt hours, or 5 kilowatt hours.

Your operating cost is, of course, also determined by your electricity cost, which can range from under 1¢ per kilowatt hour to 3¢ or more, as noted in the text. Say you pay 2¢ per kilowatt hour, and you want to know how much a new electric clothes-dryer would cost to operate. A typical dryer uses 965 kilowatt hours of electricity a year, or about 80 kilowatt hours a month (from table). It would therefore cost you about $1.60 a month to operate ($0.02 times 80). That's the average figure. It would cost more if you have a large family, particularly with small children and many diapers, less with a small family and no diapers. How to determine what you pay for electricity is given in the text starting on page 38.

The three big "swing" appliances are the water heater, range, and clothes dryer. Each of these has a voracious energy appetite, and each can be bought for use with either gas or electricity. The trick for keeping down their operating cost is to use the cheaper energy (gas or electricity) for each of them, depending on which is cheaper where you live. In some areas gas can cost as little as one-quarter as much as electricity, and in other areas electricity may be more economical. It depends on where you live. Knowing the cheaper energy can mean even greater savings when you use it for your house-heating and air conditioning.

WHAT GAS APPLIANCES COST TO OPERATE

Like electricity, operation costs for gas appliances depend on the quantity of gas used and its cost where you live. Here are average annual gas-consumption figures for the most common gas appliances in houses, according to the American Gas Association.

Appliance	Estimated Therms Consumed Per Year*
Clothes dryer, with constant pilot	93
Clothes dryer, with electric ignition	54
Incinerator, household-size	150
Range	106
Water heater	255
Yard light	167

* A therm is a quantity of gas that will give you 100,000 B.t.u.'s of heat. It is equal to 100 cubic feet of natural gas with a heating value of 1,000 B.t.u.'s per cubic foot. A B.t.u., or British thermal unit, is a standard measure of heat. It is equal to the quantity of heat required to raise the temperature of one pound of water by one degree Fahrenheit.

The operating cost of a gas appliance is figured this way. Assume you pay 10¢ per therm for gas. An electric-ignition gas dryer, the more common kind, therefore will cost 54 times $0.10, or $5.40 a year, or less than 45¢ a month. A typical gas water-heater uses about $25.50 worth of gas a year (255 times $0.10), or $2.12 per month. Remember, however, that these are average figures. Your actual cost may run higher or lower depending on such variables as how much you use each appliance. A large family will obviously do more washes and use more hot water than a small family; thus the former will have higher utility bills than the latter.

WHICH IS CHEAPER FOR YOU, GAS OR ELECTRICITY?

Gas is generally cheaper than electricity, especially if low-cost natural gas is supplied where you live. The cost of operating a gas water-heater with natural gas can run as little as one-quarter to one-half the cost of an electric water-heater—that means about two dollars to three dollars a month for gas versus six dollars to eight dollars a month for an electric water-heater. Precise figures are difficult to give because gas and electric rates vary considerably from city to city and state to state.

Natural gas costs as little as five cents per therm in the Southwest up to fifteen cents or more in New England, which is a long pipeline distance from the natural-gas fields of the Southwest. Electricity costs range from one-half cent to one cent per kilowatt hour in low-cost power areas of the T.V.A. region and Pacific Northwest to over three cents in other parts of the country, or over six times as much. (The kilowatt hour [kw. hr. or kwh.] is the standard measure of electricity.) The specific price you pay locally for gas versus what you pay for electricity will determine which is cheaper in your house.

As a general rule, if natural gas is cheaper for house-heating than oil or electricity and is therefore commonly used for house-heating in your area, gas is usually cheaper than electricity for other uses in a house. Then it will cost less to have a gas range, gas clothes-dryer, and gas water-heater. Another general rule is that gas is cheaper and more efficient for any device that produces pure, unadulterated heat. Electricity, on the other hand, is better for any device that is motor driven or electronically operated, such as a television or a radio (which, of course, is why it's universally used for such purposes).

The more equipment you have that uses one fuel, the lower your overall monthly bills will be because of step-down block rates. This means that, as an example, the more gas used each month, the cheaper it gets. Here's an example of step-down block rates from a gas company in the North:

Monthly Cost of Gas for Residential Use

Number of Therms	Cost Per Therm
First 3	$1.25 minimum monthly charge
Next 7	$0.25
Next 20	$0.12
Next 192	$0.09
Next 222	$0.08

The first small bit of gas burned each month at the above rates costs about 42¢ per therm. The more gas used, however, the lower the unit price. A gas range will use about 10 therms a month, more or less; a clothes dryer about 8 to 10; a water heater about 20. With all three using gas, you would get down to the low 9¢ bracket. If you also have gas heat, all gas burned to heat your house will cost only 8¢ or 9¢ per therm each month, and that's cheap.

Operating costs for central air-conditioning with gas instead of electricity would also be quite cheap. Central air-conditioning with gas usually costs more to install, but its operating costs can mean substantial savings, especially if you have natural gas and use a lot of it for other equipment in your house.

Incidentally, your gas company may charge you according to cubic feet of gas burned each month rather than therms. With natural gas, one hundred cubic feet of gas is equal to one therm.

Let's say that gas is the cheaper energy for you, but you presently have a mixed bag of appliances: a gas water-heater and dryer but an electric range, or any other combination. It generally will not pay to rush out and buy new equipment so everything will be on gas. The operating savings usually will not add up fast enough to offset the purchase price of the new appliance. Wait till present appliances must be replaced, and then switch to the same source of energy for each one. If you are buying such equipment for the first time or for a new house, though, by all means apply the principle of concentration for economy.

Personal preference is, of course, another consideration. You may, for example, strongly prefer cooking with electricity to cooking with gas. Then by all means fulfill your preference. It may cost you more each month, but nonetheless the extra price can be worth it in satisfaction for you. All other things being equal, however, natural gas is *generally* cheaper than electricity not only for household use but also for house-heating. Natural gas is also generally cheaper than electricity for household appliances even if oil is cheaper than gas for house-heating, and you use oil heat.

THE CASE FOR ELECTRICITY

Electricity is usually cheaper than gas for household use where it costs less than one cent per kilowatt hour. If it costs more, natural gas generally will beat the pants off of it for low monthly operating bills.

There are, however, important exceptions. A growing number of electric companies offer special low electric rates if you use electric heat or merely install an electric water-heater. Electricity can then be economical if not cheaper for household appliances because you can also get a low-cost rate break on all other electricity you use in the house. In other words, the cost of electricity for your lights and appliances often will be lower too, compared with paying the higher rate that applies without electric heat or an electric water-heater. Practically speaking, that means that electricity for all or most uses in your house can be advantageous in the following specific instances:

First, electricity has undeniable advantages if you build or buy a new all-electric house in an area where the power company gives you a low-cost break because electric heat is used. By and large, you can pay up to about 1.5¢ per kilowatt hour for electricity and it will cost little or no more than natural gas. You might even pay a little more, but electricity will save you the cost of a chimney in the new house, which can mean substantial construction savings. No gas lines must be brought to the house, and the cost of installation, service, and maintenance of electric heat is usually less than that for gas or oil heat. Such advantages can offset a slightly higher operating cost for household electricity.

Second, electricity can sometimes be advantageous in an existing house if your power company offers a special low rate if you merely install an electric water-heater. If you also use a comparatively large quantity of electricity for other purposes in your house, particularly central air-conditioning, switching completely or almost so to electricity can be economical. It's because that low rate will often extend to all the other electricity you use.

Many electric companies, for example, charge about 2¢ to 3¢ per kilowatt hour for electricity. If you install an electric water-heater, you're charged only 1.5¢, or as little as half as much. This can add up to nice savings on the rest of the electricity used each month.

Be careful of one trap, however. Some electric companies do not give you the full break on low-cost electricity with an electric water-heater. They give you the low rate only for the approximate quantity of electricity used by the water heater. The rate goes up again for all additional electricity consumed.

This depends on the company, and you must check this for yourself locally.

Step-down rates also work with electricity, as with gas. The more electricity you use, the lower its unit price. If you prefer electricity for economy or other reasons, then the more equipment you have which uses it, the better.

More specific guides for comparing the relative costs of gas and electricity are difficult to give because the cost of each varies so greatly from area to area. By knowing what you pay for each where you live, however, you can generally get a good idea of which is cheaper for you.

Some electric companies make no bones about their electricity being more expensive than gas. They promote electricity for other benefits they claim for it. Some of the benefits are indeed worthwhile, whereas others may be meaningless if not phony. For example, the nationally advertised phrase "flameless electric heat" implies that electric heat is safer than gas or oil. That's not necessarily so. More fires in houses are due to faulty electric wiring than to any other single cause.

BOTTLED GAS

Also called L.P. (Liquefied Petroleum) gas, bottled gas is the gas supplied in the cylindrical tanks often seen outside houses in small towns and rural areas beyond the range of city gaslines. In general, bottled gas will cost less than electricity for ranges, water heaters, and clothes dryers, if it costs no more than:

15¢ to 20¢ per therm, and electricity costs 1¢ per kw. hr. or more									
30¢ to 35¢ " " " " " 2¢ " " " " "									
45¢ to 50¢ " " " " " 3¢ " " " " "									

The exact balance point between the costs of gas and electricity will vary according to the family, the number of appliances used, and the local rates for L.P. gas versus electricity.

WHAT ABOUT AN OIL-FIRED WATER-HEATER?

An oil-fired water-heater is a household water-heater that is fueled by oil, just as oil is used for house-heating. The oil water-heater is, off and on, aggressively promoted by fuel-oil dealers. You'll sometimes hear that if you already have oil heat, you can save money on an oil water-heater, too. This is, by and large, not true. Gas water-heating is usually cheaper, especially with natural gas. The electric water-heaters are also beginning to give oil a run for its money where electricity is coming down in cost.

Besides, an oil water-heater must be serviced and adjusted once or twice a year, or its efficiency runs down, and operating costs go up. The initial price and installation cost of oil water-heaters also run more than those for either gas or electric ones. An oil water-heater is worth considering only if you live in an area with no city gas-mains and you have oil house-heat or if electricity is expensive where you live and bottled gas is expensive or difficult to get.

TWENTY-ONE COST-SAVING TIPS

Your monthly utility bills can also be reduced by getting the most out of your equipment and avoiding waste. This may sound obvious, but it often is not. Pay special attention to the appliances that eat up big chunks of gas and electricity, as noted in the tables on pages 24–25 and 26. For example, an electric-range oven accidentally left on overnight will use up to twenty to thirty times more electricity than a light bulb left on overnight.

Here are twenty-one specific tips from home economists and other experts on how to avoid waste and get more for your utility dollar. Some may sound elementary, but they're included because they are common causes of waste, and not everybody may know about them. Other tips are not so well known, and still others may or may not be practical in your house.

1. Run your dishwasher, clothes dryer, and clothes washer only with a full load. Putting each through a full cycle for a partial load is costly because you still pay for virtually full-load power.

2. Don't overdry with a clothes dryer. Overdrying is the greatest single cause of harshness, shrinking, and wrinkling of fabrics. It shortens clothing life and therefore increases your clothing bills.

3. Set the water-heater thermostat down to the lowest temperature of hot water needed. This is usually the hottest faucet water your hands can tolerate. Too high a setting means excessive fuel consumption, and extra cold water is needed from the faucet to cool it down. The water heater ordinarily can be set at about 140° F. Experiment a little to get the lowest hot-water temperature that is satisfactory. Sometimes, however, you must compromise because the dishwasher or clothes washer requires water of 160–180° F. Otherwise, the dishwasher may not do a real cleaning job on your dishes.

4. If extra-hot water is required for your dishwasher, although all other household water need only be about 140° F. or so, a dual-supply valve can be put on your water heater by a plumber. It divides the water-heater supply into two circuits: extra-hot for the dishwasher and other such equipment and ordinary hot water for all other use.

5. When you build or buy a new house or remodel your present house, remember that a separate water-heater with its own tank usually is more efficient and less expensive than having your faucet water heated by a coil built inside the house-heating boiler (as is sometimes done with hot-water heat). A separate water-heater with its own tank is also less likely to run out of hot water when you need it most (during a shower, for example). It can be run by gas, electricity, or oil.

6. Insulate long runs of hot-water supply piping from the

water heater to the house. This usually can be done at the basement ceiling, where such piping is exposed. Good pipe-insulation
can be bought from a mail-order house such as Sears or Mont-
gomery Ward or from a hardware store.

7. Locate a new water-heater as close as possible to the kitchen
and bathrooms. This will mean short piping and reduced hot-
water pipe losses. This is easy to do with an electric heater
because it doesn't have to be connected to the chimney like a
gas or oil heater. It can be located in any dead space close to
kitchen and bathrooms.

8. Roast meat at temperatures no more than 325–350° F.
Roasting at 450° F. uses 20 to 30 per cent more heat and
greatly increases meat shrinkage. Roasts cooked at no more than
350° F. generally taste better, too.

9. Prevent violent boiling by turning the heat down when
cooking. A slow, rolling boil cooks just as quickly and saves
fuel; it also reduces heat and humidity in the kitchen. (An
exception is cooking pasta, which requires fast, violent boiling.)

10. Load the oven as much as possible. A number of different
foods often may be cooked simultaneously, which saves fuel.
Don't overload, however, or you may have to turn the temperature up. Some kinds of oven use, such as baking, must of
course be limited to one item.

11. Broil with your broiler-compartment door closed. Most
broilers are designed for closed-door cooking, which saves fuel
and reduces kitchen heat.

12. Avoid frequent oven peeking. Opening the oven door
wastes time and fuel, which nearly every woman should know.
A range with an oven light and a window can make opening
a door unnecessary.

13. Use pots and pans with tightly fitting lids to prevent the
escape of steam (and also vitamins).

14. To get maximum performance from an electric range, use
flat-bottomed, straight-sided pans that make full contact with
the electric heating-element. Some modern electric ranges have
patterns that can be adjusted to the pan size being used.

15. Don't locate a refrigerator or freezer next to a heat-producing appliance such as an electric range or dishwasher. The heat generated makes the cooling equipment work harder and longer.

16. Don't allow a lot of frost to build up in the refrigerator. A wall of frost acts as an insulator, preventing efficient refrigeration. The motor must run longer and uses more electricity.

17. Make sure the clothes dryer has a moisture exhaust duct from its rear end to the outdoors. A dryer should not dump its exhaust inside the house. That can exert a greater load on the dryer, possibly lengthen the drying time, and require more heat. Also, moisture discharged into the house, even in the basement, can lead to expensive structural damage.

18. Keep the lint filter inside the clothes dryer clean. The lint should be removed after every drying cycle. Excessive lint prevents a free flow of air, and the dryer must operate longer. It also can create a fire hazard.

19. Don't leave an appliance turned on when you're finished with it. The worst offenders include electric cooking-elements left turned on inadvertently after you have removed cooked food, an electric coffee-maker left simmering all morning long, and, among other things, the hair dryer left on unthinkingly. Being human, almost all of us do such things occasionally, but making yourself aware of the energy consumed can reduce such wastage. It can also avoid an expensive disaster from things like burned-up coffee-makers or hair-dryers, more than one of which have started house fires.

20. When you rewire your house, have pilot-light switches installed for garage, cellar, and outside lights. A small red bulb on the switch lights up when the light is on, thus telling you that the light in the cellar or outside wasn't turned off. That signals you to switch it off when it's no longer needed.

21. Pay your bills on time. This can save you money because of the discounts offered by some utilities for quick payment or by avoiding the penalty for paying late. In one large metropolitan area you can save 10 per cent on water and electric bills and

4 per cent on gas bills by paying when the bills arrive. That can save you two to three dollars a month, which isn't peanuts.

LIGHTING AND LIGHT BULBS

Money can be saved, of course, by turning off unnecessary lights, but don't worry too much if an occasional bulb is left on all night. You haven't wasted that much money, though former President Lyndon Johnson made news by going around the White House at night, putting out lights. That was a costly practice for a man paid more than thirty dollars an hour (over fifty cents a minute). A trainload of one-hundred-watt bulbs would have had to be turned out to compensate for the President's time. A sixty-watt bulb left on all night only uses about one cent's worth of electricity. A batch of lights continually left on is something else again.

You also do not save much by skimping on light-bulb sizes, using a sixty-watt bulb, say, when a one-hundred-watt size is necessary for adequate light. Light bulbs should be chosen first of all for the amount of light required and secondly according to the effort required to replace it. Don't skimp, particularly in dark areas where good illumination is needed. Use a big-enough bulb to see well. A dim light could lead to a nasty fall and a heavy sock in medical bills, compared with the small change saved on electricity.

Long-Life Bulbs

These are well suited for places that are difficult to reach to replace the bulb. That would be, for example, a fixture on a high ceiling, which requires hauling out a ladder to reach the bulb and replace it. A long-life bulb ordinarily will last twice as long as a regular bulb (1,500 hours versus 750).

The savings on such bulbs, however, are lower than many

people think. In addition, long-life bulbs give less light than a regular bulb of the same wattage, particularly in sizes above 60 watts. Long-life bulbs are therefore recommended only when you need 60 watts or less of light, in addition to their suitability for hard-to-reach locations.*

Fluorescent bulbs, on the other hand, give considerably more light and illumination per watt than regular incandescent bulbs. That makes them especially economical where you need light for long periods. A pair of 20- or 30-watt fluorescent bulbs, for example, can give you the same illumination you would get from a 100- to 150-watt incandescent bulb, with considerably less electricity used. Fluorescent bulbs also last longer.

CHECKING YOUR MONTHLY BILLS

How much gas and electricity should you use each month? Has the company made a mistake? (Sometimes it does.) Is there a quick and easy way to check each bill without laborious (and boring) computations?

The quantity of gas and electricity used each month obviously depends on the number of gas and electric appliances you have. A typical family will use between three hundred and five hundred kilowatt hours of electricity a month. That's for lighting, the usual complement of small appliances, and perhaps an electric washer. If you have an electric dryer and/or an electric water-heater, you might use from six hundred to one thousand kilowatt hours a month. Electric heating in the winter can increase that substantially.

---

* After the above was written and just before this book went to press, new long-life electric bulbs were introduced by several companies, including Duro-Test and Westinghouse. These new bulbs are said to be good for as many as 2,500 hours of operation, versus the usual 750 for standard bulbs. Whether or not these bulbs do that and overcome previous drawbacks of long-life bulbs are things yet to be determined. Try a few, if you wish, and match them against the performance obtained from regular bulbs. Maybe long-life bulbs have finally arrived.

Electric heat for the average family in the North will use about three thousand to four thousand kilowatt hours of electricity during a cold month. In summer a three-ton central air-conditioning system will draw up to fifteen hundred to two thousand kilowatt hours of electricity a month. It can be a little more or less, depending on the house, family, and climate.

Gas consumption for a typical family generally runs about ten therms (one thousand cubic feet of natural gas) a month for cooking and another twenty to twenty-five therms more or less for a gas water-heater, as indicated earlier in this chapter. A gas clothes-dryer will add another ten therms, more or less, and gas heat in winter will by itself burn about three hundred to five hundred therms of gas a month during cold winter weather. Again, the exact consumption depends on such variables as the house, family heat requirements, and local climate.

How Much Do You Pay for Gas and Electricity?

Determine this from your actual bills and from the electric company's rate card. Note on a bill the quantity of electricity used for the month as well as the charge for it (less any tax added on). The electricity used will be the meter-reading at the beginning of the month subtracted from the reading at the end of the month, or "present reading" minus the "previous reading."

Say the result is 414 kilowatts of electricity used for which you are charged $11.80. You paid 2.85¢ per kilowatt hour ($11.80 divided by 414), the bill in dollars divided by the electricity used. This figure will vary a little from month to month (or every two months, as bills are sometimes sent), but by and large, it will stay within a steady range.

Your actual cost for gas is figured the same way; i.e., divide your total gas bill in dollars by the quantity of gas consumed, as noted on your bill. Assume you used 197 therms of gas during the month, to pick another figure out of the air, and your bill is $20.43. Your gas cost is therefore 10.4¢ per therm, or per one hundred cubic feet of natural gas ($20.43 divided by 197).

Knowing the price you pay for gas and electricity can tell you the approximate operating cost of adding major new equipment such as air conditioning to your house. It can also tell you how much can be saved by switching from gas to electric equipment or vice versa or from gas to oil or oil to gas heat.

Checking Your Bills

"Is this bill right?" "There must be some mistake." Those are typical reactions when the monthly bills come. Usually the bills are right, though mistakes are sometimes made. If, by the way, nobody was home to let the meter man in when he came, the company will use an "estimated" reading to figure your bill for the month. It will be corrected the following month when your meter is read.

Checking a bill requires step-down arithmetic and a copy of the rate schedule in each case. Here's how it's done for an electric bill. Assume that you used 414 kilowatt hours of electricity for the month and the local cost of electricity is as follows:

Number of Kw. Hrs.	Cost Per Kw. Hr.
First 13	$1.25 minimum charge
Next 47	5¢
Next 51	3¢
Next 714	2.2¢
Over 825	1.5¢

Your bill is figured like this:

The first 13 kw. hrs. cost you	$ 1.25
The next 47 kw. hrs. @ 5¢ cost	2.35
The next 51 kw. hrs. @ 3¢ cost	1.53
The remaining 303 kw. hrs. @ 2.2¢ cost	6.67
The total charge is	$11.80

Gas and water bills are checked the same way, though the units are different.

Charting Your Bills

This is the quick way to check bills. Keep a record of your monthly bills for gas, electricity, and water, as shown on pages 42 and 43. It gives you a running record of both the charge and the quantity of each used each month. With it a new bill can be quickly compared with recent months and with the same month last year and the year before. You will quickly see if the bill is in line with other comparable months. You can also quickly see without a lot of arithmetic whether the charge is right. This is done by your table, which will show the price charged at other times for approximately the same quantity of gas, water, or electricity.

There are other advantages to recording your monthly utility bills: A sudden rise in gas, water, or electric use can mean that something's wrong. It can mean, for example, that the water heater is getting old and inefficient, requiring increasingly large amounts of power to heat water; it might need service or replacement.

An unknown water leak may have occurred, causing a continuous loss of water which you're unaware of. The author of this book once noticed that his water bills had mysteriously increased. Checking back bills, I found that our family normally used about 8,500 gallons of water a month, but now we were using (and paying for) 11,000 to 12,000 gallons of water a month. No change in family habits, such as increased lawn-sprinkling, explained the higher bills. Something was wrong.

We looked into things around the house, and, sure enough, a faulty toilet-tank mechanism (a common cause of leaks in houses, by the way) was found in the upstairs bathroom. Water was silently leaking out of the tank continuously, day and night. New water was continuously being supplied inside the tank to offset the constant loss. The mechanism was fixed, which stopped the leak. The water bills returned to normal after a loss of more than 15,000 gallons of water over a period of several months.

Your monthly record of your bills can also help you determine the cost of heating or cooling your house. It can help you estimate whether or not it would pay to buy storm windows to cut fuel bills in winter, increase the house insulation, or take other such steps to reduce heating and cooling bills.

Your bill records can also shed light (as well as point out potential savings) on questions about the purchase of new appliances and equipment. We've mentioned that merely determining your actual cost for gas or electricity can help you estimate the operating cost of a new appliance you might buy or determine whether or not switching to an electric water-heater and lower electric rate would return worthwhile savings. When you expand or improve your house, it can help you decide whether a separate new gas- or electric-heater would be better and less expensive for that new room or rooms.

A record of monthly bills can be kept with tables like those shown in this chapter (pages 42 and 43). The quantity of gas and electricity used each month is noted with the total charge for each. If your gas or electric bill is mailed out every two months, your table is adjusted accordingly. The quantity of gas and electricity used is recorded in addition to the price because the electric company may change its rates. You will then pay more or less than before for the same quantity of gas or electricity used. Knowing how much electricity was used in the past is then a more telling figure than past bills in dollars.

Monthly Bills for an Actual Family

The accompanying utility-bill tables for an actual family also show how the monthly use of gas and electricity can fluctuate from month to month and year to year.

The figures are the actual bills received by the author and his family (one wife, three children) while living in a two-story Victorian house in a suburban area approximately twenty-five

Electrical Bills for a Typical Family

		Jan.–Feb.	Mar.–Apr.	May–June	July–Aug.	Sept.–Oct.	Nov.–Dec.
1968	Kw. hrs.	1684	1417	1299	2841	2319	1843
	Cost	$42.18	$36.54	$33.95	$59.54	$51.71	$45.93
1967	Kw. hrs.	1538	1338	1285	1322	3488	1570
	Cost	$39.60	$35.20	$34.03	$34.84	$69.28	$39.91
1966	Kw. hrs.	1490	1331	1600	2950	2259	1558
	Cost	$42.40	$38.43	$45.15	$68.50	$58.14	$40.04
1965	Kw. hrs.	1368	998	1192	2286	1882	1110
	Cost	$39.49	$30.10	$34.95	$62.30	$52.20	$32.90
1964	Kw. hrs.	1176	1262	1417	2289	1832	1154
	Cost	$34.69	$36.84	$40.72	$62.52	$51.09	$39.14
1963	Kw. hrs.	1242	766	712	1990	1756	988
	Cost	$38.22	$26.32	$24.97	$55.04	$49.19	$29.29
1962	Kw. hrs.	1124	1074	878	1608	1388	994
	Cost	$35.27	$34.02	$29.12	$47.37	$41.87	$32.02
1961	Kw. hrs.	1132	954	724	1583	1808	795
	Cost	$35.47	$31.02	$25.27	$47.61	$52.37	$27.05
1960	Kw. hrs.	676	590	480	1008	1876	774
	Cost	$24.07	$21.92	$19.17	$32.37	$54.07	$26.52

Gas Bills for a Typical Family

		1968	1967	1966	1965	1964	1963	1962	1961	1960
Jan.	Therms	567	414	451	397	357	520	530	618	126
	Cost	$47.50	$38.99	$42.00	$39.00	$32.79	$55.00	$55.00	$67.00	$19.00
Feb.	Therms	378	411	408	518	498	494	523	464	
	Cost	$35.05	$59.03	$39.00	$49.00	$43.99	$51.00	$54.00	$51.00	
Mar.	Therms	258	292	186	130	270	228	253	354	114
	Cost	$24.77	$28.57	$21.00	$16.10	$27.60	$23.00	$28.00	$40.00	$18.00
Apr.	Therms	129	193	235	200	287	195	206	282	
	Cost	$14.22	$20.38	$24.64	$22.16	$30.00	$20.00	$23.00	$32.00	
May	Therms	106	130	174	182	83	163	108	166	98
	Cost	$12.11	$14.65	$19.29	$20.07	$11.00	$18.00	$13.00	$20.00	$17.00
June	Therms	40	31	30	32	47	34	44	91	
	Cost	$6.89	$5.52	$6.07	$6.30	$8.00	$6.00	$8.00	$12.00	
July	Therms	100	14	49	76	13	90	40	60	87
	Cost	$11.79	$3.50	$7.83	$10.42	$4.00	$11.00	$7.00	$9.00	$16.00
Aug.	Therms	13	13	13	13	21	13	35	13	
	Cost	$3.48	$3.37	$3.48	$3.50	$5.00	$3.00	$7.00	$4.00	
Sept.	Therms	59	45	79	91	145	74	97	60	96
	Cost	$8.06	$6.73	$10.62	$11.68	$17.00	$10.00	$13.00	$9.00	$17.00
Oct.	Therms	84	110	124	131	185	100	169	178	
	Cost	$10.39	$12.54	$14.82	$14.48	$21.00	$12.00	$20.00	$21.00	
Nov.	Therms	233	567	222	279	196	301	293	280	362
	Cost	$29.96	$50.22	$23.66	$28.42	$22.00	$28.00	$33.00	$31.00	$45.00
Dec.	Therms	389	286	309	271	442	477	544	430	400
	Cost	$36.66	$27.94	$30.41	$27.72	$43.00	$42.00	$58.00	$45.00	$45.00

43

miles northwest of New York City. The location has an average northern clime of about 5,000 degree days a year for house-heating. The house has 1,750 square feet of living area. In 1960, the first year shown, the family used gas for cooking, water-heating, and house-heating; electricity for the washing machine, clothes dryer, and a 2.6-ton central air-conditioning system. The cost of gas and electricity were the rates shown on pages 28 and 39.

Notice how the bills reflect a modernized kitchen done in February, 1964. A new electric range replaced an old gas range, and a dishwasher was installed for the first time. Subsequent electric bills rose, and the gas bills declined. Gas heat was installed in October, 1960, replacing oil heat, which explains the low bimonthly gas cost earlier in 1960.

The figures also show fluctuations in gas for heating and electricity for cooling from year to year. The high electric bills for the summer of 1967 was because that was one of the hottest summers of the decade. The cost of heating the house was $200 to $235 a winter (September to May); central air-conditioning cost from $65 to $75 a summer (June to September). These figures were extrapolated from the tables by subtracting the average gas and electricity used for all other uses during the same periods from the totals per month.

The tables hold a few discrepancies. They're due to such things as the family being away on vacations for two to three weeks in March, 1965, and February, 1966, the cost of gas reduced a bit in early 1966, and the cost of electricity reduced by 5 per cent in November, 1966.

An interesting mistake was made in early 1966 when the author replaced an old gas water-heater (which died then) with a new gas heater. If a new electric water-heater had been installed, savings would have been realized on subsequent electric bills. A new electric water-heater would have reduced the cost of electricity to 1.5¢ per kilowatt hour for all power used over 408 kilowatt hours bimonthly. An electric water-heater was not installed because the author did not realize at that time that such savings were possible and was not then keeping a record of his bills. The tables shown were compiled later from old bills.

REDUCING WATER BILLS

This section can help you eliminate common causes of water leaks and heavy water wastage.

A faucet drip, the most common water leak, is deceptively wasteful. A single faucet dripping off and on can waste two hundred to three hundred gallons a month. If it's leaking hot water, your water-heater bill also rises. The cure is simple, usually requiring only a new faucet washer. What's not so simple, of course, is overcoming inertia and getting the job done. The job generally takes only a few minutes and can be done by nearly anyone, as described in Chapter 4.

A toilet drip will waste even more water and money. Ordinarily it is stopped merely by jiggling the toilet handle. You figure that will take care of things until you get around to fixing it. Again, the problem is chiefly human inertia; before the drip is fixed, considerably more water has been wasted than you might think.

The kind of hidden toilet-leak noted earlier in this chapter will not respond to jiggling the handle. The tank fills up, but water continuously leaks out the bottom. This can sometimes be detected by eye or ear. You will see water dribbling continuously into the toilet bowl in between flushes. Sometimes, though, it can be a very subtle leak, with nary a ripple, and not easily detected.

If you're suspicious, put a small quantity of dye into the top of the tank. Don't flush. If the water in the bowl below shortly becomes discolored by the dye, there's a leak. The dye seeping down gives it away.

The leak may be caused either by too high a water level inside the tank or by a faulty ball-seal at the bottom. The first is remedied merely by adjusting the water-level arm to a lower height. The second generally requires a new ball, which is cheap, obtained at a hardware store, and easily installed. You unscrew the old ball and screw on the new one. It's a good idea to dye-test a toilet periodically.

Other Water Economies

Use an economical shower-nozzle. All shower nozzles are not alike. Some spray as little as two gallons of water per minute, others up to ten gallons a minute, or five times as much. Medium ones spray about five gallons a minute. Obviously, a small output is the most economical, especially if one likes to soak himself long and gloriously in the shower. You may want a medium nozzle or shower-head to satisfy your minimum spray needs, but a large size is ordinarily both unnecessary and wasteful.

The spray rating should be noted on the shower head. Whether or not it is, does your shower spray seem greater than necessary? If so, a new shower-head with a known rating can be picked up in a hardware or department store or at a plumbing-supply house for as little as three or four dollars. The best kind comes with an adjustable spray and a volume control. That lets you adjust the spray from a gentle rain up to a full-flooding cascade for rinsing your hair. It also lets you cut the water volume down to the minimum required.

If you have a water conditioner, be sure that it bypasses the cold water used for the lawn outdoors and other such purposes. In some houses it's also easy to connect the softener so that it bypasses the cold water supplied to the bathroom toilets too, another large user of water that certainly does not need softening. Sometimes merely connecting the softener to the hot-water supply will meet your needs and avoid unnecessary water-softening for the bathrooms and outdoors. You can buy salt for a softener in large quantities at low cost, but avoid the very cheapest salt, which could foul the conditioner.

An automatic clothes-washer can use a lot of water. Some models use as little as twenty gallons of water a load, others more than forty. The difference obviously can add up. Remember this when you buy a new clothes-washer.

SUMMARY

Monthly utility bills can be reduced. The best way is to concentrate the costliest appliances to operate—range, water heater, and clothes dryer—on the cheapest fuel. Remember this when you must replace one of these appliances.

If you use great quantities of electricity, particularly with central air-conditioning, you can often save by going completely or nearly so to an all-electric house, assuming that you will get a low-cost break on electricity by installing an electric water-heater.

Watch your bills. Keeping a record of them can be revealing, especially when and if they show a sharp change from the norm.

CHAPTER 3   HOW TO REDUCE TELEPHONE
BILLS AND SAVE ON LONG-DISTANCE CALLS

■ *Avoiding charges for wrong numbers, and other mistakes . . .*
Choosing the lowest-cost monthly service . . . Special billing
plans with more calls for your money . . . Reducing monthly
charges for optional equipment (special phones, extensions, etc.)
. . . Saving on long-distance calls . . . Person-to-person versus
station-to-station calls . . . Reducing individual-call charges
and overall monthly bills . . . Buying low-cost, privately made
telephones . . . Money-saving tips.·

GOVERNMENT FIGURES show that the telephone bill is now the
largest single utility expense for the typical American family.
It has edged out electric bills for that distinction, though telephone rates rose comparatively little during recent periods of
galloping inflation.

We use the telephone more and make many more long-distance
calls, particularly since direct-dialing long-distance came in and
made it so easy. Many of us, however, have become profligate
with the telephone. For example, we make calls indiscriminately,
requesting an operator to make a call for us when the charge
may be considerably less if we dialed ourselves. Here are some
important ways to reduce your telephone bill:

   ▪ Get credit for a wrong number or the times when you are
cut off and must dial again.

   ▪ Choose the most economical monthly billing plan for your
purposes. This means, among other things, knowing which local
calls are "free" and which cost you money.

   ▪ Know how long-distance charges work, which means more
than knowing that calling at night or on a weekend is cheaper.
That, in fact, is not always true.

- Know the difference between long-distance charges for calls within your own state and those to another state.
- As a general rule, make station-to-station rather than person-to-person calls.
- Don't go overboard for auxiliary equipment that costs you extra money every month.

WRONG NUMBERS AND CUTOFFS

You are charged for a wrong number automatically unless you call the operator and request a credit. You're also charged when you are cut off in the middle of a call and must redial for a new connection. Again, you must notify the operator in order to receive a credit.

Telephone-company officials expect such mishaps to occur in about 10 per cent of all calls dialed, so don't be shy. To avoid charges on your bill, let the operator know when one of your calls misfires. Not doing this can cost you more than you might think.

A California woman we know of, for example, was prone to dialing mistakes and did not realize that when dialing friends in Los Angeles, whose area code is 213, she would sometimes get New York, whose code is 212, or Chicago, whose code is 312. You're almost always charged for a minimum three-minute call, and the computer automatically charged her each time for an expensive long-distance call.

If you get a wrong number, notify the operator. Operators are instructed to record the credit at once. Keep a record of such mishaps. Note the number wanted and the time and date called. Check each against your bill later to be sure you were not charged extra. If you were charged by mistake, call the company. You'll get the credit on your next bill. Be particularly alert to wrong numbers that could cost you the price of a very-long-distance call. You could accidentally get a distant city when you're merely calling nearby.

YOUR MONTHLY BILL

Your basic bill depends on the type of service and the number of local calls made. You are charged extra for all calls dialed beyond your local calling-area—usually an area within a certain radius of your home. Beyond that radius, the farther the call, the higher the charge.

An "unlimited-call" or "flat-rate" service is usually the best and cheapest. You pay a basic monthly charge of about six dollars to seven dollars a month. You may dial any number of local calls and talk as long as you wish on each call. The "local calling-area" for unlimited calls usually includes certain nearby telephone exchanges, which should be described in the front of your telephone book. It's good to know them, for a call to any other exchange costs you an additional sum on top of your basic monthly bill.

If you make comparatively few local calls a month, you can save a little money by asking for "message-rate" service. You're allowed fifty to seventy-five calls a month for a dollar or two less per month than an unlimited service. You pay extra, though, for each additional call over the monthly minimum.

A party line can save a dollar or two a month, though it's not available all over. It's recommended, however, only for people on a tight budget who are willing to share their phone line with others. There are two- and four-party-line services, this last being the cheapest but also the most restrictive, of course.

More Calls for Less Money

A family that makes many calls every month outside of its local calling-area can sometimes save money by taking advantage of a special billing plan. For example, the monthly bills for one large family in an eastern suburb regularly included charges for 150 to 200 message units in addition to their basic

$5-a-month service. (A message unit usually costs five cents and is used to gauge the price of calls in a given area. Each call is charged in message units, according to its distance. Additional message units may be charged for extra time on the phone. A call ten miles away may cost you 2 message units for the first three minutes, an additional message unit for each additional minute or two on the phone.)

The family paid about $10 a month for those extra calls on top of their basic $5-a-month bill. They learned that the same number of message-unit calls could be had for $5 a month with an extended-service billing plan, called Call-Pak in some areas. They continue to get unlimited local calls ($5 a month) and up to 200 additional message units ($5 additional charge), but they save $2.50 to $5 a month on roughly the same total number of calls as before. A plan like this can save you money if you make many calls outside of your immediate area.

Though not available all over, another optional plan may give you a break if you make a number of calls beyond nearby areas but within your state during the month. In one state it's called the Econ-o-call plan (another tongue twister from the telephone company). It gives you a discount, in effect, on frequent calls made within the state. It has four variations, depending on the number of calls. You get:

(A) Up to $3 of calls for $2.50 minimum charge per month, save 50¢
(B) Up to $6 of calls for $5   minimum charge per month, save $1
(C) Up to $12 of calls for $10   minimum charge per month, save $2
(D) Up to $24 of calls for $20   minimum charge per month, save $4

You must, however, pay the minimum charge for the plan selected even if you make fewer calls in a month. This plan will save you money when you consistently run up more than $2.50 in state-wide calls each month; the greater the number, the more you can save. This plan is added on to your basic billing-plan. It does not affect the cost of local calls.

Which plan is for you? The different billing services described may or may not be available where you live, and in some states other services may be available. That's because there are twenty-four different telephone companies in the Bell System, each of which runs its own show. In addition, there are—hold your breath—some two thousand independent telephone companies outside of the Bell System. Each of the fifty states also has its own telephone rules and rates. Things are by no means uniform.

The optional plans generally available are usually, though not always, noted in the front of your telephone book. To be sure, call the local business-office to determine what may be new and economical for you. A particular plan obviously may or may not save you money, according to your phone use. If you choose a plan and it does not save you money, you almost always can drop it. Check this, however, with the company beforehand.

SAVING ON LONG-DISTANCE CALLS

The charges made and the savings possible depend first on whether a long-distance call is made within your own state or to another state. The charges for long-distance calls within a state vary for the reasons mentioned above. The savings you can make by waiting till evening also vary, and sometimes there are no savings.

In New York, for example, the charge for a call up to forty-four miles away within the state is always the same, day or night, Saturday, Sundays, and holidays. There is no need to put off such a call just to reduce the cost. The charge for a call farther away is reduced after 6 P.M. on weekdays and all day Saturday, Sunday, and holidays. If the call is more than forty-four miles away but less than seventy-one miles away, there is no further reduction; if the call is seventy-one miles away or more (still within the state), there is a second reduction after 8 P.M. and all day Sunday. The savings can range from five cents to perhaps one dollar or more if you wait till 8 P.M. or Sunday to make a call.

Specific facts about long-distance charges within your state will be found in your telephone book, or if they are not listed, call the telephone company.

Out-of-State Long Distance

The charges and savings possible on out-of-state calls are uniform throughout the country. They are set by the Federal Communications Commission (F.C.C.) and are handled by American Telephone & Telegraph's Long-Lines Department. But they are not, alas, simple and uncomplicated, so bear with us as we unravel them—or try to.

All long-distance charges on calls between any two states are based on the airline mileage between the two points, but the cost of a three-minute call from Bangor, Maine, diagonally across the country to San Diego, California, a distance of 2,668 miles, can be as little as 70¢ or as much as $3.30, depending on factors other than distance. That's also the price range for a call from Los Angeles to New York (2,452 miles) or from Portland, Oregon, to New Orleans (2,070 miles).

Such calls cost the most on weekdays between 8 A.M. and 5 P.M. and when they are made person-to-person. A person-to-person call means, of course, that the operator gets you a particular person by name; it's the most expensive kind of call at any time. The charge for a person-to-person call of 1,911 miles or more (between New York and California, for instance) is $3.30 for the first three minutes, 45¢ for each additional minute. (These and all other rates given in this chapter do not include tax charges. And some or all of the rates may be raised or lowered at any time.)

Long-distance charges change according to the type of call, distance, and time the call is made. For example, a three-minute station-to-station call between New York and California on a weekday is $1.70. A shorter-distance call, made to a place a mere 70 miles away but also in another state, costs 45¢ for three minutes.

A three-minute long-distance call is cheapest of all from 8 A.M. to 11 P.M. on Saturday and from 8 A.M. to 5 P.M. on Sunday. Remember this last point—it's cheapest on Sunday only up to 5 P.M. The maximum charge for a long-distance call (up to 3,000 miles away) that you dial yourself during these times on Saturday and Sunday is 70¢ for three minutes and 20¢ for each additional minute. Charges for shorter-distance calls during the same periods drop according to the smaller mileage.

If you cannot wait till Saturday or Sunday to make a call, you generally can save during the week by calling after 5 P.M. Now things can get even more complicated.

For example, sometimes you can save more by waiting till 11 P.M., but this only works for calls to points more than 354 miles away. (This odd mileage is used because of intricate formulas of the kind that make life simple and bearable only for certain lawyers.) In general, you save the most during the week on calls made after five in the afternoon. The additional savings possible on calls made after 11 P.M. are often no more than 5 or 10 per cent on a three-minute call, with one exception. The exception is a special late-night, one-minute rate of no more than 35¢ for the longest long-distance call (within the United States). This special rate goes into effect every night at 11 P.M. until 8 A.M. the next morning. It's for brief phone calls you dial yourself. The maximum charge of 35¢ for the first minute plus 20¢ for each additional minute applies to all calls 1,911 miles or more away (e.g., East to West Coast). The charge is less for shorter calls (25¢ for a one-minute call from Chicago to either Miami or San Francisco or the other way around plus 20¢ for each additional minute). The one-minute charge applies to all long-distance telephone calls from one state to another. It can not only save you money on brief calls but it can also be useful if you live in the West and want to call east before eight in the morning at your house.

Nonsaving Calls

No savings are made on certain calls by waiting till after five in the afternoon. This means that you can make certain long-distance calls at virtually any time day or night, weekday or weekend, without worrying about paying more. The rate is the same at all times. These are calls to another state up to fifty-five miles away; cut-rate charges for such calls virtually never apply. The charge is the same in the evening and late at night, on weekends and holidays, and during prime calling-time on a weekday, so there's no need to postpone such a call to save money.

Don't be put off by the involved mileages and different time periods you must know to save the most on telephone calls; they are, to be sure, complicated and varied. You can beat the system simply by making a little table of your own for the cities you call the most, and by noting on it the best times for making calls to each.

Person-to-Person Calls

A few special words about person-to-person calls. They are expensive. The charge for a three-minute, person-to-person call can be nearly three times as much as the same call dialed direct, station-to-station. It's because an operator must handle a person-to-person call, whereas direct dialing is done automatically (with nonunion electronic equipment).

A good rule is dial direct, station-to-station, when there is a fifty-fifty or better chance of the person you want being near his telephone. Even if he takes a minute or so to get to the phone, the call will be cheaper than person-to-person. It also can be cheaper if he isn't there. You may need only to leave a message for him, request that he call you back, or inquire when he will be there so you can call back. Then the cost of the two calls can still be less than the cost of one person-to-person call. If you get him on the first call, you're ahead of the game. This is illustrated in the following table of typical long-distance charges.

Long-Distance Telephone Charges between New York City and Chicago (or between Any Other Two Cities 675 to 925 Miles Apart)

Time at Calling Phone	Station-to-Station Call				Person-to-Person Call	
	Dialed Yourself		Operator Assisted Call, or from Coin Phone			
	First 3 Minutes	Each Additional Minute	First 3 Minutes	Each Additional Minute	First 3 Minutes	Each Additional Minute
DAY Monday to Friday 8 A.M. to. 5 P.M.	$1.15	$0.35	$1.45	$0.35	$2.40	$0.35
EVENING 5 P.M. to 11 P.M. Sunday to Friday and all day on holidays	.65	.20	1.10	.25	2.40	.25
NIGHT 11 P.M. to 8 A.M. every night	.50 or .20 for one minute	.15	1.10	.25	2.40	.25
WEEKEND Saturday all day but only 8 A.M. to. 5 P.M. on Sunday	.50	.15	1.10	.25	2.40	.25

Long Distance Reviewed

The greatest savings can be made by holding off nonurgent calls till Saturday or during the day Sunday. Savings on more important calls generally can be made by waiting till five in the afternoon or till seven in the evening, depending on the distance called. Whenever feasible avoid the high charge made for person-to-person calls no matter when they're made and dial direct.

Because the costs of both in- and out-of-state calls vary according to the time of the call, find out the charges for the calls you frequently make. If they're not listed in your telephone book, call the telephone company for them. A company representative may even type a list of the charges for calls to cities you frequently phone. Put the list near your phone, and it can save you money.

Like the old Model T Ford, the cheapest telephone is a black one. Unlike the Model T, a variety of optional equipment can be had for a phone, and you pay extra for nearly all of it. Some entails a monthly rental charge on top of your basic bill, other equipment requires a one-time installation charge but no rental charge, and some things have both kinds of charge. Such equipment can subtly build up in expense. It may pay to reappraise your need for what you have now, particularly if you want to reduce your basic monthly bill. You may save money with little or no loss of convenience.

For example, the installation of a telephone jack or two around the house is cheaper than an extension telephone. A portable phone is plugged into a jack where the phone is needed. A jack has a one-time installation charge and that's it, whereas each telephone extension has a rental charge every month.

Here are the approximate charges for various optional equipment. The charges will vary a bit from state to state, so you may pay a little more or less than these prices.

Each telephone extension: $1 to $1.50 per month plus installation charge

Colored telephone: installation charge of $5 to $7, usually no monthly charge

Princess phone: 75¢ to $1 a month plus installation charge

Trimline phone: $1 to $1.25 a month plus installation charge

Bell chimes: 75¢ to $1 a month for all phones in the house, usually no installation charge

Touch-tone phone: $1.50 total a month for one or more with the same number, usually no installation charge

Those charges are for a private residential telephone service. The same equipment for a business number costs more.

Your total cost for optional equipment may be difficult to determine, because it's not itemized on your bill. To find out, call the telephone company. If such equipment is no longer wanted, it will usually be removed at no charge.

BUYING YOUR OWN TELEPHONE EQUIPMENT

An antique phone you buy yourself or an ordinary privately made telephone used as an extension may not save you the monthly rental charge for a company-phone extension. Such equipment is now permitted by law, but it must conform with telephone-company standards "to avoid operating problems," A.T. & T. points out. Thus a telephone you buy must usually be modified to be electronically compatible with the telephone company's dialing equipment. The telephone company will as a rule do this for a one-time charge, perhaps ten to thirty-five dollars, depending on the work required. It must be done for most antique phones on the market which plug into a regular telephone-company jack.

In addition, you must also pay the standard monthly rental charge for your own phone, just as if it had been rented to you by the telephone company. That's why you generally will not save money with your own equipment. Its chief value is the pleasure and satisfaction you may get from an antique phone or from one of the internationally admired Ericofons.

You can, of course, buy your own telephones to use as extensions without telling the telephone company. Eventually, however, a routine test of local lines would very likely tell the company that strange equipment is in use. You would be requested to have it adapted to their standards at the going price or remove it. If you have it adapted and keep it, you would then be billed the regular rental charges made for such equipment. If you refuse, the telephone company can legally suspend your service. Not everyone agrees with such rules, which someday may be challenged in the courts. Until they are successfully challenged, however, you do not save money with your own telephone equipment.

OTHER WAYS TO SAVE

▪ Check your telephone bills. A wrong number you reported may have gone unrecorded. An expensive long-distance call may have been mistakenly charged to you (though sometimes it's a call you want to forget, especially after seeing the charge). Reviewing your bills also can reveal changing patterns in your telephone use and call attention to expensive calls to be avoided in the future.

▪ Time your long-distance calls. Use a three-minute egg timer or ask the operator to tell you when your three minutes are up. After your first three minutes—in some cases four minutes—the little meter in the company computer starts clicking away, charging you minute after minute.

▪ Plan ahead before making a long-distance call. Think out beforehand the purpose of your call, exactly what you want to say, and, possibly, what you want to learn. If a knotty problem arises during the call, let it ride till afterward rather than waste expensive time while the meter's going. Politely cut your call off and say you'll call back when you've solved the problem.

▪ Use local "tie-line" telephone numbers. They're often provided by stores and others you deal with who require a toll call from you: that means a department store, airline, and such people as Sears Roebuck, who may be located a 25¢-call away from you. Using their tie-line telephone number lets you dial them at no charge to you. In some areas it's an "Enterprise" number; that's the exchange you dial. The other party pays for your call to encourage your business. Various departments of the city, state, and federal government also do this, particularly those which use the phone a lot (it cuts down their telephone cost, too). Many national companies also have tie-line numbers to call from city to city, though these are generally restricted to their own people.

▪ Eliminate the charge for an unlisted number. An unlisted telephone-number ordinarily adds a monthly charge to your bill. You can kill this charge simply by having your number listed under the maiden name of a wife or other such name unknown to most people. Have the telephone company send the bill to that name care of you at your address.

▪ Get a telephone-company credit card. It can be highly useful for calls you make away from home. You merely give the operator your credit-card number, and the call is charged to your home bill. It permits calls away from home without having to search for the right change, and it also gives you a record of such calls for business reasons. You request the card from the telephone company. You need not carry it with you; just remember the number. It is basically your home number plus a few digits.

▪ Keep abreast of special billing plans offered by the telephone company. They are usually announced in the advertisements sent with your bill. Like many people, you may automatically consign such advertising to the nearest wastebasket without a reading. You should, however, scan such material before tossing it out. Check the front section of a new telephone directory each year for a new plan that could reduce your monthly bills.

▪ Review your telephone use periodically. Telephone needs change as time goes by. When children reach the talky teen-age stage, your telephone often gets increased if not indefatigable use, and you get record bills. When the children leave home, the pattern can be reversed. A different, more appropriate billing plan may serve you better at less cost. If your bills simply seem unnecessarily high, don't shy away from calling the telephone company about a possible alternative service that can meet your needs at lower cost.

CHAPTER 4 HOW TO AVOID HOME-REPAIR
BILLS

■ *Avoiding expensive service calls for common appliance problems*
. . . Preventing breakdowns of clothes washers, dryers, and TV
sets (which call for the most frequent service) . . . Tips on
small and large appliances . . . How long appliances last . . .
Avoiding house structural repairs and emergencies . . . Pre-
ventive maintenance for plumbing, termites, wood rot, wet
basements, leaky roofs . . . Reducing repainting costs . . .
Dealing successfully with repairmen.

A WOMAN called a repairman to come by and fix her family's TV
set, which had stopped working. She urged him to come quickly
because her kids naturally considered a blacked-out TV a virtual
national catastrophe. It took the man a couple of days to arrive—
among other things, he had a prior list of other TV sets to be
cured—but when he did, he had this one working in jig time. It
was an easy ten-dollar service call. All he did was push the TV
cord firmly back into its electric outlet. The picture lit up immediately. The cord had been jarred loose apparently by a child
or the family dog.

That may sound bizarre, but it happens frequently. You still
must pay the minimum charge for a five-dollar-an-hour repairman
and his five-dollar-an-hour truck (fairly low rates today, which
soon may be as extinct as the dodo). The charge also covers the
man's time to your home and back to his shop.

"As many as 50 per cent of all home-repair calls can be
avoided," says George W. Johnston, president of Allied Home
Owners Association, a Long Island, New York, home-service company. Many service calls and repair bills can be avoided simply
by going down a brief list of standard check items before calling
the repairman, just as an airline pilot goes down his checklist be-

fore taking off. A small problem will often be found and can easily be corrected by any reasonably intelligent man or woman. You need not be a mechanical genius, and these are stitch-in-time preventives that can forestall king-size breakdowns and repair bills later.

Sick appliances of one kind or another account for the biggest single service expense in residential America today. Since the end of World War II Americans have bought close to one billion major home appliances, and sooner or later most must be fixed. For every dollar spent on appliances, it's estimated that we spend another twenty to twenty-five cents to service them. We spend another seven or eight billion dollars a year on repair work for our houses, which means such things as fixing the plumbing or wiring or doing something effective (and for good, we hope) to clear up a wet basement.

BEFORE CALLING THE REPAIRMAN

When an appliance breaks down, pause for a moment and consider what might be ailing. Is the switch turned on? Are the controls set properly? Is the electric plug firmly in the socket? Perhaps there's no electricity because the fuse has blown at the main electric board. Plug another appliance that is working into the outlet to test for power, or if necessary, replace the fuse. If you have circuit breakers, you need only push the "off" one back to "on."

If a fuse or circuit breaker continues to blow, there's a short circuit somewhere. It could be in the appliance that is giving you trouble, especially if the fuse does not blow when the appliance is unplugged, or it may be in some other device plugged in on the same electric circuit. A little experimenting, plugging in the other devices one at a time, will usually tell you which one is the culprit. Some equipment will have its own built-in fuse or circuit breaker operated by a protruding red button. Push the button firmly, and that may get things running again.

Sometimes the problem is in the electric cord or with an exten-

This electric service board distributes electricity from the power coming into the house to individual house circuits. Electricity to any house outlet is turned off simply by pushing the circuit breaker—one of twenty black switches lined up in front of the board here—to "off." Either you or your electrician can write next to each switch which rooms and appliances are controlled by it. All house electricity can be turned off by the master switch at top. If the board has fuses, a burned-out fuse must be replaced. If this frightens you, turn off the main-board switch first, and turn it on when the fuse is replaced (also reset your electric clocks). BETTER HOMES & GARDENS.

sion cord you may be using, not with the appliance. An extension cord can be easily checked by trying it with another appliance that is working. A loose wire at one end or the other may be shorted or broken. Nearly any person can repair or replace a bad cord with a screwdriver. This may seem a forbidding job to some people, but the alternative is usually spending twice the time finding a repairman and three times the cost to pay for the mending.

The instruction booklet that came with the appliance often will tip you off to other common causes of trouble. If you don't have one for an appliance, write the manufacturer for it before trouble occurs. Specify the model and serial number of your device. Not every manufacturer's instruction booklet, to be sure, is very good. Some are superficial, inadequate, or just plain worthless, which can leave you dangling (though you could squawk to the maker— if enough people do this, threatening to avoid his products in the future, he may make improvements).

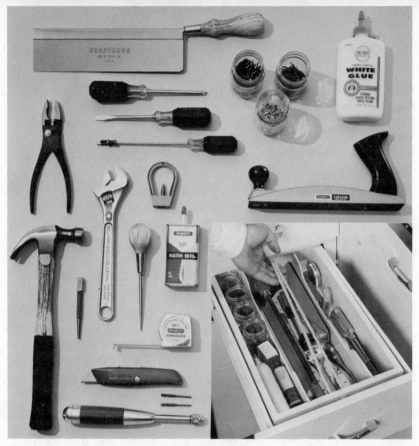

The basic tools shown here will enable a person to handle many repairs. They include a dovetail saw, pliers, screwdrivers (including Phillips type), nails, an assortment of screws, all-purpose glue, a multi-bladed forming plane, a hammer, a set of nails, an adjustable wrench, a stud finder, an awl, an oil can, a tape measure, a shop knife, a push drill, and drill bits. BETTER HOMES & GARDENS.

Portable box (insert) *permits tools to be carried easily.* BETTER HOMES & GARDENS.

Here are some common causes of failure for household appliances and equipment that tend to require the most service.

Clothes Washer and Dryer

If appliances in general account for the most repair bills in residential America, the clothes washer and dryer drain off more repair money than any other appliances. If the washer or dryer stops working, make the standard first checks recommended for most problems. Be sure the electric plug is pushed in firmly and that the fuse has not blown. Check the controls, each one separately, and whatever else is suggested by the manual for your model. If it's the washer, be sure that the hot and cold water faucets are turned on. Is a water hose kinked or a hose strainer clogged? Is the loading door open? Some washers have a safety switch that will stop the machine if it is open. An overload or out-of-balance load will often stop the machine. The overload reset button may have to be pushed in to start the unit again. Too many suds and twisted hoses together with overloading are frequent causes of breakdowns. Another common problem is a coin, a bobby pin, or even a wristwatch bobbing up inside the washer and causing havoc with the internal mechanism (not to mention what happens to the watch). Overloading can cause premature motor failure and a major repair bill, so avoid this operating shortcut. The small extra time and cost of a second wash, instead of overloading, and the time to clean out pockets of clothing beforehand is well worth taking to avoid the replacement expense of a broken drive-mechanism. And turn off the water faucets between washings. Keeping the water supply on when not in use keeps constant pressure on the machine. It can weaken the valves.

If the clothes dryer doesn't start, check the controls, and be sure the door is snapped closed. With a gas dryer be sure that the pilot light is on and that the main valve is also on. If the clothes take too long to dry, the lint trap may be clogged or the exhaust vent blocked. The lint trap should be cleaned after every use.

Television Set

If the TV set is dead, again be sure the plug is square in the outlet and that the house wiring is in order. Be sure the antenna wires to the back of the unit are firmly wired to their terminals, and that the bare wires of the antenna wire don't touch one another. If the picture has excessive snow or the sound is weak and noisy, your antenna may be facing the wrong direction or the wires to the house may have come loose from the antenna. Be careful, though, if you must go on the roof.

If you have a picture but no sound, adjust the fine tuning control with the volume control turned all the way up. Try another channel or two. If only one channel is not showing properly, it could be the station transmitter, so allow time for correction. If the sound is normal but the picture is gone, turn the brightness control on fully and try another channel.

Heat is a major enemy of TV sets, and the great heat generated can break down internal components. Be sure, therefore, that there is plenty of air circulating around your set. A set should not be put against a wall or in a corner with little air circulation.

Vacuum Cleaner

Government home-economists have found that dirt-clogged vacuum cleaners are the greatest cause of service calls. Empty your bag often, they say, and don't let the bag get packed solid. That sharply reduces dirt pick-up ability and also strains the motor. If dirt gets into the motor itself, usually as the result of an overloaded bag, the motor will overheat and run down. If the motor labors or feels excessively hot, it's usually time for the bag to be emptied or replaced.

If your unit uses disposable bags, it's best to use only the manufacturer's replacement type especially made for your machine. A substitute off-brand type may give a poor fit and allow dirt to get into the motor.

Dishwasher

The most expensive dishwasher repairs result from broken glass, which can jam a pump mechanism and burn out the motor. If a dish breaks inside, turn off the machine and pluck out the broken pieces before they cause damage.

If your unit makes peculiar sounds, labors, or just does not function properly, ⬛⬛⬛ ʋ. ⸰ it or pull out the fuse or turn off the electricity at the circuit breaker; then look down into the inner mechanism. You'll have to remove the trays, of course. Use a flashlight, and remove any debris with pointed-nose pliers, if necessary.

If your dishes do not come out clean enough, it's usually because the water isn't hot enough. It should be at least 140–150° F., though check the instruction manual to be sure. It also could be the wrong detergent or wrong amount of detergent being used. Sometimes a rinse additive is needed. Some makes and models work considerably better than others. If your dishes do not wash as clean as those of a friend or neighbor, it could simply be the difference between the effectiveness of the two machines. All that we can suggest is that you get a better machine next time.

Refrigerator

Most refrigerator trouble occurs on hot and humid days when the unit must work the hardest to keep things cool inside. You may see vapor coming from the refrigerator and think it's smoke, which it sometimes may be. Usually it is merely water vapor due to the high humidity. It generally means that the refrigerator needs a good cleaning.

The walls inside of a double-temperature refrigerator should be washed every week or two, or a thin film will form that collects moisture and dampens operating efficiency. Don't let frost build up more than a quarter of an inch thick. Defrost regularly as needed.

A noisy refrigerator may have a loose grill behind or a loose drain pan underneath. The condenser coils at the rear or bottom of the unit should be brushed or vacuumed regularly. Also be sure that air can circulate around the condenser coils. This means, among other things, that a refrigerator, like the TV set, should not be enclosed in an unventilated corner of a room. Air must be allowed to circulate freely behind it.

If your unit seems to run more than necessary, double-check

the little condenser pipes in the back, and make sure they are clean. Be sure the doors close firmly against their gaskets. Close the door on a piece of paper. If the paper pulls out easily, the seal is bad and thus permits air leakage. You may need a new gasket, or the door hinges may have to be tightened.

Check your instruction booklet for the periodic maintenance your refrigerator may require. Some brands, for example, should have their drains checked and cleaned several times a year. Most of the suggestions given here also apply to freezers.

The Range

If the oven of an electric range does not heat, be sure the timer is on "manual," not "automatic." Check the controls to be sure each is set not only properly but firmly in. Movable elements should also be plugged firmly in place, or they may not heat.

With a gas range be sure that the pilot light is on. If a gas burner heats unevenly or incompletely, some of the orifices may not have dried thoroughly after being washed, or they may be clogged and require cleaning. Clogged parts can be opened with a small wire or a paper clip. After washing allow for drying before cooking.

Small Appliances

Most small appliances are relatively trouble-free except, of course, for the shoddiest, poorest-quality ones. Avoid poor quality and, if necessary, pay a little more for good quality when you buy.

A dry iron that stops working will generally need a new thermostat, coil, or heating element. There is little you can do but replace the defective part. Steam irons are less troublesome, although they may get clogged, especially if you have hard water. Clean out the sediment periodically. Automatic-toaster repairs usually involve replacing a thermostat that has gone bad. (That's what controls the degree of toasting and the pop-up mechanism.)

GENERAL TIPS

The life of appliances can be prolonged and breakdowns minimized by applying an occasional drop of oil here or there, cleaning the equipment periodically, and making an occasional readjustment. Specific recommendations should—again—be noted in the instruction booklet. An appliance dealer or repairman can also give a few such suggestions (though not all are as helpful or as articulate as we would like).

Whenever possible take a broken appliance to the repair shop. This can save you money compared with the extra cost of paying a man and his truck to come to your house. Before taking a bulky appliance to the repair shop or before requesting a serviceman to call, however, ask the man on the phone if he might suggest what could be wrong. Tell him the symptoms of the illness, just as you would tell a doctor. Tell him about possible strange noises and how the equipment acted just before the breakdown. Often this will ring a bell with a good repairman, and he will have an idea of the likely problem and whether you might handle it yourself.

However, don't necessarily tell a repairman what you think is wrong. One woman told a TV serviceman that she believed the picture tube was broken. That's all he needed to know. He charged her for a new picture tube although a relatively minor defect was the real cause of trouble. Just say how the device is misbehaving, and let the man determine why and what's needed. If a major new part is required at hefty expense, also say that you want the old part back when it is removed. A reliable serviceman will do this without being asked. If you're dealing with a new serviceman, it's a check on his honesty.

Also never tell a repairman to go ahead and fix something without first getting an estimate of the approximate repair cost. An example of what too often happens is the woman who left a vacuum cleaner to be fixed, just saying she wanted it to work again. The bill came to $46.70! A new vacuum of the same kind, then on sale, would have cost $49.50. Get an estimate before you tell a man to fix a broken appliance regardless of whether you have taken it to his shop or he has come to your house, or tell him to go ahead and fix it if it will cost no more than, say, five dollars. Otherwise he should let you know how much the repairs will cost before he fixes it.

By and large, it's best to have repairs done by the people who sold the appliance to you or at the manufacturer's service center or one of his franchised service dealers. A list of such places is usually included in the package with a new appliance. Factory service centers are often listed in the yellow pages of the telephone book. Look under the kind of appliance involved.

In general, repairing an appliance does not pay if the repair cost exceeds 50 per cent of the price for a new one. That's a rule of thumb, though, not a dictum. If it is comparatively new, a high repair bill may be worthwhile, since it should have renewed life and last a long time. If, on the other hand, the device is old and not long for this world, you will do well and save money to boot by junking it and buying a new one. That goes for old appliances even when the repair cost is sizable but less than 50 per cent of the price of a new model.

The approximate number of years of service you can expect from appliances is given in the following table. The figures can

Appliance	Average Years of Life
Clothes dryer	14
Clothes washer, automatic and semiautomatic	11
Clothes washer, wringer and spin dryer	10
Freezer	15
Range	16
Refrigerator	16
Sewing machine	24
Television set	11
Toaster, automatic	15
Toaster, nonautomatic	7
Vacuum cleaner, upright	18
Vacuum cleaner, tank	15

tell you approximately how much life is left in your appliance and thereby indicate whether or not repairs are worthwhile when they may be needed. This is the average life of typical household appliances, according to a United States government study. Of course, the same equipment lasts longer for some people and less time for others. Longevity will depend on the quality of the appliance, how well it is maintained, and the amount of use it gets. The figures are chiefly for electric appliances, though the figure for kitchen ranges covers gas, too.

HOUSE STRUCTURAL REPAIR

Appliance repairs may occur more frequently, but a single major repair to the structure of your house can dwarf appliance repairs in magnitude and repair cost. Just as a car requires periodic service to keep it running well, a house and its various structural parts can also use a certain amount of periodic care and maintenance. You'll benefit by a sharp reduction in the likelihood of a major repair bill, by possibly avoiding a major emergency headache, and by getting better service and satisfaction from your house. Here are the most common structural problems encountered in houses, the best ways to prevent them, and common breakdowns that can be fixed by nearly every homeowner.

Plumbing

Problems with sinks, drains, faucets, and other parts of the household plumbing circuits are generally second only to those with appliances in producing household-repair bills. The most frequent problems are caused by clogged drains, septic-tank breakdowns, and leaky faucets. The first two can largely be avoided by simply not using the kitchen drain as a flush for food, fats, oil, grease, coffee grounds, and other such insolubles (though food can be handled by a kitchen-sink garbage-disposal unit). Don't use the toilet for a trash can, or you're inviting trouble.

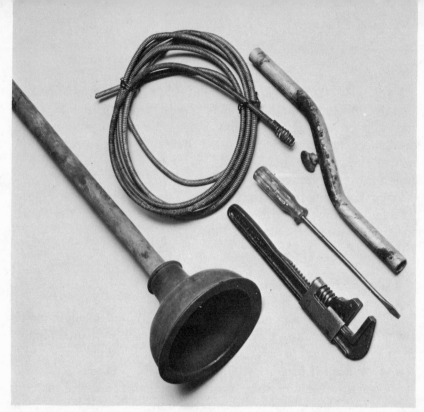

Here's all you'll need to handle most plumbing drain problems, probably the most common and frequent annoyance to plague homeowners (and apartment dwellers, too): a plunger ("plumber's friend"), a wrench, a screwdriver, and a spring-type wire "snake" with an adjustable handle for reaching down into pipes to dislodge a blockage. BETTER HOMES & GARDENS.

That means sanitary napkins, paper towels, and the like should be disposed of elsewhere; they are as hard on a septic tank as sand on an automobile engine. Even with a city sewer, the same bulky waste can clog your sewer and require an expensive plumbing call to open it up again.

Most faucet leaks are caused by a worn-out washer inside the faucet. They are a continual problem in most houses, as well as a source of wasted water and high water bills. Nearly anyone, including a nonmechanically inclined person, can replace a worn washer and fix a leaky faucet. It takes a few basic tools—screwdriver, pliers, and an adjustable wrench and ten to fifteen minutes of time. You can save the five to ten dollars that a plumber gets to do the same thing.

You shut off the water valve to the faucet, unscrew the faucet handle, and disassemble the faucet piece by piece until you come to the worn washer. Replace it, and assemble the faucet in the reverse order. A box of assorted washers can be gotten at a hardware store and should be standard operating inventory in every house. With a single-lever faucet special parts may be required. Consult your plumber (by phone), a hardware-store man, or visit a plumbing-supply house. Tell them the brand and model you have, and you should be able to get the parts needed.

If you're tackling things like a faucet washer for the first time,

A faucet drip can be fixed with these few tools: assorted washers, screws (which come with the washers), a screwdriver, a reseating tool, and packing thread. Shut off the water and remove the faucet stem and washer (held in hand). The worn washer is removed with the screwdriver, and a new one is installed. If the washer seat is rough, the reseating device, costing about one dollar, will smooth it. If water leaks around the faucet stem, tighten the packing nut or remove the old packing and wind a new packing into place. AMERICAN WATER WORKS ASSOCIATION.

you should have a good home-handyman's book as an aid. It can tell you how to cope with a great variety of household repairs. Three of the best are *America's Handyman Book*, by the Family Handyman Staff, published by Charles Scribner's Sons in a revised edition for $10.00; *Better Homes & Gardens Handyman Book*, by the editors of *Better Homes & Gardens*, published in paperback by Bantam Books, Inc., for $1.25; and *How to Fix Almost Everything*, by Stanley Schuler, published in paperback by Pocket Books, Inc., for 75¢ (the hard-cover edition is published by M. Evans & Company, Inc., for $4.95). Any bookstore can supply one of these books, which will be well worth its price; they are also available from many libraries.

Plumbing Precautions

Remove the shower nozzle-head in a bathroom (you just unscrew it in most cases), and brush and clean it periodically. Remove and clean kitchen-sink drains, especially the pop-up kind. Put a good cleaner down the kitchen and bathroom drains periodically. Turn off the outside water-faucet every fall and drain its supply pipe to prevent freezing and broken pipes in winter.

If your plumbing drain-line from the house to the street (called the soil pipe by plumbers) runs under a big tree or two, it could get clogged by the trees' roots. They can stop up the pipe and cause a major plumbing stoppage (and an awfully messy emergency). It's a common problem. Porous tile pipes beneath old houses attract roots to them like ants to a picnic. Roots can be discouraged from strangling your sewer line if you periodically drop blue copper-sulphate crystals down your toilet drain the last thing at night. The crystals can usually be had from a hardware store or from a druggist, or order "Rootox" pills from a Sears, Roebuck catalog.

If you have septic tank or cesspool, it should ordinarily be pumped out about every three to five years—more frequently if you have a garbage-disposal grinder. A good septic-tank-cleaner powder can also help the system function better.

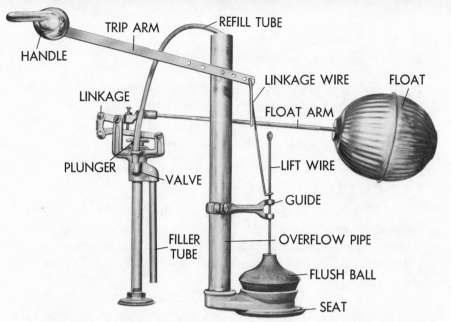

TRIP ARM REFILL TUBE

HANDLE

LINKAGE WIRE FLOAT

LINKAGE

FLOAT ARM

PLUNGER

VALVE

LIFT WIRE

GUIDE

FILLER TUBE

OVERFLOW PIPE

FLUSH BALL

SEAT

The profile of a typical toilet flush-tank looks like this. If the tank does not fill up, it's usually because the flush ball doesn't sit well in its seat—adjust its functioning, or replace the ball. If the tank fills but water continues to run, adjust the float arm down to attain a lower water level. Other problems can ordinarily be diagnosed simply by removing the tank cover, tracking down the malfunction, and correcting it. It's usually quite easy. BETTER HOMES & GARDENS.

Avoiding an Emergency Flood

You could avoid a major catastrophe if you know where several key things in your house are located. Do you know, for example, the location of the central water shut-off valve for your house? If a water pipe breaks and a bad leak springs up, this valve should be turned off fast. You'll avoid the predicament of a family whose plumber, confronted with an emergency leak, spent hours hunting down the main shut-off valve. No one knew its location. He finally found it only after removing large sections of basement paneling. The homeower paid dearly for an expensive treasure hunt.

If you have a septic tank or a cesspool, know its location too. Another man had to have his front lawn virtually completely dug up for a plumber to locate his flooded septic tank. The house waste had backed up and it started flowing again only after the septic tank was found and pumped out. An underground septic tank or cesspool can generally be located from blueprints of the house, which everyone should have if possible, or by asking the builder, architect, or previous owner of your house.

Avoiding Termites

If you live in a termite area, a termite inspection is recommended at least once a year. Termites are found in nearly every state of the United States nowadays. If in doubt about their prevalence where you live, call your county agent at the county office building.

The inspection should ordinarily be done by an expert, which means a termite exterminator. A reasonably observant and interested homeowner can learn to do the inspection himself. It will help if you first take a guided tour of your house with a hired termite expert. He looks carefully for veins of mudlike dirt—termite tunnels—which range from about one-quarter inch to as much as a foot wide. To an inexperienced eye, they look deceptively like streaks of ordinary dirt and are easily overlooked. That's what termites want you to think, since they swarm in droves, in paradelike fashion, in and out of the house through their ingenious dirt tunnels.

An expert will also jab house timber with a knife to detect termites at work under the surface. Window frames and floor and basement beams and posts (particularly near ground level, where they are the most vulnerable) get the knife test. An expert will do this during a step-by-step inspection of the outside of a house and the interior foundation and basement walls.

Don't be complacent if your house has termite shields or if you live in a house with a concrete-slab floor and no basement. Some of the worst termite destruction has occurred in houses with shields; termites can beat them and often do. If your house has a concrete floor, inspect the plumbing access-hole regularly. This is the floor opening for pipes, usually behind a panel in the bathroom. It's a popular point of termite entry into the house. Cracks in the slab and in the foundation walls should be plastered over with cement.

Don't let raw earth (dirt) pile up against the wooden skirt of your house. Keep at least six inches of clearance between the lowest wood of the house and the ground. Don't store firewood in or near the house. Dead wood is a magnet for termites, and it's an easy jump from the wood to the house. Firewood stored in or near the house also can be a magnet for other wood parasites such as carpenter ants, which can be as bad as termites. Use a wood-shed or other storage area well away from the house.

Avoiding Wood Rot

This causes even more damage nationwide than termites. It's the result of moisture soaking into wood of the house anywhere from cellar to attic. A fungus attacks damp wood, causing it to rot and decay. It's sometimes called dry rot, but that's a misnomer that has arisen because rotted wood often looks dried-out.

To prevent wood rot, your house structure must be kept well ventilated and dry. That means keeping the wooden skirt of the house free of the encroachment of damp ground soil, as recommended for termite prevention. The entire basement structure, spaces under a porch, a crawl space, and the attic should also be kept well ventilated and dry the year around.

For this reason attic vents should not be closed in winter. If your attic floor is insulated, the loss of heat from the house will be inconsequential. A closed space, such as those below outside steps and porches, should be aired with vents to keep it dry. Be sure that no water or rain can get in, since water is the eternal enemy here.

Drying Out a Wet Basement

A dry basement is important for several reasons. In addition to the mildew and ordinary puddle and odor problems arising from water in the basement, the water compounds the likelihood of

This splash block steers roof-water drainage away from the house walls, and it will often avoid a wet basement. It prevents water from seeping down to the foundation walls. Its cost is about two dollars to three dollars per ready-made block; the same drain control can be easily made at no cost with properly shaped stones or bricks. PORTLAND CEMENT ASSOCIATION.

both termites and wood rot. The overt symptoms of a wet basement are all too visible—water dripping down the basement walls and pools of it on the floor. On the other hand, things may look dry, but inescapable dankness in the air signals the presence of water that may not be apparent at first glance.

About half the time, basement water is caused by rain that does not drain away from the house. Water pools up next to the house, sinks into the ground next to the foundation, and then pushes through into the basement. Get the water to drain away from the house on all sides, and this will often lick the wet basement problem. Fill up low spots around the house walls with new dirt. Tamp it down, sloping the earth away from the house on all sides. That should keep rain draining well away from the basement.

Sometimes the problem is roof leaders (vertical drainpipes from the roof to the ground) that do not drain their water away from the house, or from those that go underground and get clogged up; in the second instance the water backs up and into the ground and oozes into the basement. If your roof leaders drain into underground pipes, be sure that the pipes are not clogged, particularly if your basement is wet nearby. Test the drain by uncapping it above the ground and running a stiff wire down into it as far as you can probe. Better still, flush water from a hose down into it. If the water soon backs up, you've got a clogged pipe. If the pipe can't be cleared, disconnect the roof-leader pipe from it, and let the leader spill its water onto the ground, where it can be directed away from the house.

If the basement water does not stem from poor outdoor drainage or a bad roof-leader, it's usually due to wet ground and poorly waterproofed foundation walls. This sometimes can be solved with good waterproofing compound or paint applied to the interior of the basement walls. Sometimes a minor water problem can be handled simply with a dehumidifier or water pump in the basement which gets rid of the water as it comes in.

If, however, you are unfortunately and chronically bedeviled by a really bad wet-basement problem, the ultimate solution may require a complete waterproofing job around the outside surface of your basement walls. A trench must be dug around the house, and a system of in-the-ground drainpipes is generally needed at the exterior base (the footings) of the foundation walls. This can get expensive, but it is sometimes the only effective way to cure a chronic wet-basement problem. It may be less expensive if only one wall is the chief source of your water problem.

Roof, Gutters, and Leaders

The first sign of roof trouble is usually a damp spot on the ceiling or high on a wall inside the house. It's a leak. It's time for action. A bad leak sometimes, but not always, may mean you need a new roof.

Many leaks are caused by overflowing roof gutters (the wood or metal channels around the roof eaves which carry off rainwater), by a broken metal flashing-collar where the chimney goes through the roof, by the flashing in a roof valley, or merely by a bad roof-shingle or two.

Check the roof gutters first. If they are clogged and filled with leaves and small branches, clean them out and keep them flowing. The gutters usually require cleaning in spring and fall. You'll need a hose, a stick to pry matted leaves loose, a ladder, and a casual attitude toward height. Wooden gutters should be given a coat of roofing asphalt or linseed oil every two or three years to prevent rot.

Be sure that the vertical leaders from the roof to the ground are clear and flowing. If water does not flow down the leaders, you'll have to pry out the obstruction with a stiff wire or take the leaders apart section by section to locate the obstruction. If the leaders drain underground and out of sight away from the house, the obstruction could be in the underground section, as noted earlier.

If the roof gutters and drains are clear and flowing, the metal flashing around the chimney (where the chimney goes through the roof) or other flashing near the leak should be checked. Sometimes the leak can be spotted by stains under the roof in the attic. Plugging the leak depends on how much of—and how willing—a do-it-yourselfer you have in the family and, alas, whether or not a whole new roof is required.

Leaks in roof flashing often can be stopped by coating the flashing with roofing asphalt, which is bought at a hardware or

Roof leaks often occur around chimney and pipe vents, the first places to look for them particularly before you buy a new roof. Cracks in the chimney flashing are sealed with roofing cement. Large gaps should be renailed shut.   BETTER HOMES & GARDENS.

paint store. This little job often can keep you going for several years before a new roof is needed. (It did just that for five years for the author of this book before he had to capitulate and pay for a new roof.) A roof that is clearly old and worn-out, however, should not be ignored too long. Facing up to a new roof, although it is a painful expense, can put an end to continual leaks, ruined plaster, and ugly wall-stains inside the house as a result of spreading leaks. Call a few roofers for their opinions as well as their estimates for a new roof.

Most roofing requires surprisingly little maintenance, considering the savage beating that a roof takes from the hot sun. There's one notable exception. That's a roof of wood shingles or shakes. Left to themselves, they'll eventually dry up, curl, crack, and go to pot. Give them a therapeutic rubdown off and on with a cedar roofing-preservative to keep them happy. One or two coats every four or five years are usually necessary. A good roofing-supply dealer can recommend a good formula, and a roofer can apply it at comparatively reasonable cost. The Federal Government recommends a creosote oil with the "full-cell process," which "will

A heavy coat of roofing cement is brushed on the roof joint around the pipe. The joint between the outer pipe-sleeve and a vent pipe should be sealed.
BETTER HOMES & GARDENS.

greatly prolong" wood-shingle life. The next best thing is a creosote and coal-tar preservative brushed or sprayed on. Frequency of treatment depends on your climate and such variables as the kind of wood, the roof pitch, and the treatment applied to the shingles when they were first put on. A local wood-shingle supplier or roofer can also tell you the frequency recommended in your area.

Outside Walls, Woodwork, and Repainting

Paint is thought of as a cosmetic treatment by some people—simply something to keep your house looking nice. The paint you put on is also the only thing that stands between the wood and the weather, and when that protective film of paint fails, things underneath will go bad fast.

Besides, the best way to cut down the cost and frequency of repainting a house is to use the very best and longest-lasting paint and have it put on properly. The cost of the paint is a very small portion of the total repainting cost, and the extra cost of the very best quality paint over that of ordinary quality is small. If a painter does the job for you, it is sometimes better for you to provide the paint. Its cost is then deducted from his total charge. A top grade of latex paint is usually best of all nowadays. Resist the urge to compromise at the time of purchase just to save a dollar or two per gallon. That can mean the difference between house paint that will last three or four years and really good paint that will last up to ten years.

Repainting and repairs to the outside of your house also can be reduced by inspecting the house every spring and fall and catching worn and damaged spots before they grow serious. Cracks around window and door frames should be caulked. (Incidentally, the new plastic caulking will last many years longer than old kinds of cheap caulking.) Cracks and holes should obviously be patched before they grow. The hinges of roto-operators on windows should be oiled. The channels of sliding windows should be cleaned with steel wool.

Take a stroll around the house every once in a while, and check on such things. Of course, the human tendency is to put off all but emergency repairs that won't wait, but if you can muster up a burst of energy and occasionally spend a few hours or so mending minor trouble when you first spot it, you'll save yourself considerably more repair work later or the equivalent in money charges paid to a repairman. The same periodic inspections are recommended even if you have aluminum siding or any other low-maintenance, long-life kind of walls on the house. In such cases, repainting will still be required for the house woodwork (windows and doors). Woodwork, by the way, accounts for a sizable portion of the overall job when a whole house is painted. Take this into account when you consider the virtues and savings of having new aluminum siding installed on your house to eliminate the cost of repainting. You'll only save the cost of painting the house walls. The woodwork still must be repainted just as often as before. (More on aluminum siding is given in Chapter 8.)

When to Do Your Own Repairs

You will save the most money on jobs with the highest labor cost. A plumber, for example, may charge five dollars or more to fix a leaky faucet, but the only part ordinarily required is a two-cent washer. The rest of the cost goes for the man's time, again usually including getting to and from your house. Do the job yourself, and you save virtually the whole bill. And as we have indicated more than once, the job often can be done in less time than that required nowadays just to get a repairman.

Other jobs with a high labor-to-material cost-ratio include replacing broken window-glass, caulking door and window frames, cleaning and replacing the furnace and air-conditioning filters, repairing a faulty toilet-tank mechanism, replacing a broken porch-step, and putting a new plug or complete new electric cord on a broken lamp or small electric appliance. The cost of labor accounts for well over 90 per cent of the repairman's bill for each of these jobs and others like them. Usually only a few basic tools are required for such jobs. Armed with a good handyman's how-to-do-it book, nearly anyone can do them. Getting the chores done can also give you a feeling of satisfaction and achievement, even if it is not a world-shaking accomplishment.

. . . And When Not To

It's best not to tackle repairs on complicated machinery such as a dishwasher or clothes washer; definitely do not attempt anything that requires probing into the high-voltage anatomy of a TV set—unless, of course, you're a mechanical expert. Also steer clear of major repair work on plumbing, heating, and air conditioning. Electrical problems can also be dangerous unless you've learned well about wiring or you're tracking down a wiring problem in an appliance that can be unplugged first or one in which the wiring circuit can be switched off dead while you're probing around.

Dealing with Repairmen

"What! Twenty-seven fifty for that little job?" It's said all the time, but your squawk may or may not be justified. There are good and honest repairmen and also those who are neither, just as there are good doctors, lawyers, and other such skilled and capable people and those who are not so good, to put it mildly.

Often the key to good service at an honest price is establishing a good relationship with reliable dealers and servicemen. Stick with the same men, and they'll usually stick by you when they're needed. When you buy an appliance that is likely to require service, evaluate the service you'll need *before* buying. It is generally best to buy only from a dealer who can provide the service, preferably with his own service department. The quality of the service provided should be a major influence on your decision.

When a new appliance is delivered, be at home to receive it. Be sure to get an instruction booklet with it. Have the installation

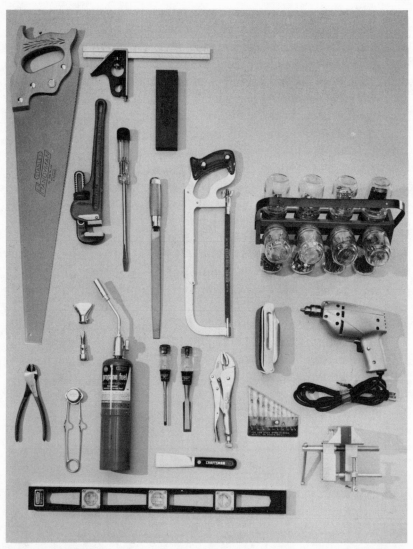

A basic array of tools like these will truly put you in business—they're recommended for the man who really wants to be prepared. Besides the more recognizable implements, included are a sharpening stone, a pipe wrench, and a deluxe propane torch with varied tips. BETTER HOMES & GARDENS.

man review its operation and give you a few tips on maintenance and avoiding a breakdown. Be at home when a repairman comes, or at least have someone meet him with the service instructions and other information you may have for the equipment he's come to fix. This can be invaluable to a repairman and save him time and you money. Getting out your TV set instructions, for example, will usually provide the man with a wiring diagram of your set. This can help the serviceman quickly track down an obscure little gremlin that would otherwise be an elusive quarry.

The foregoing may sound as if you must go into the household-repair business virtually full-time to keep up with household repairs nowadays. Actually, a family will be confronted with only a small portion of these problems over a period of years, but applying a little preventive maintenance around your house as recommended can sharply reduce your problems. This means applying the ounce-of-prevention principle. The nice thing about it is that, in all, it will require no more than a few hours of your time every once in a while. Consider those few hours of time an excellent insurance-premium which can someday spare you literally days and weeks of travail with a major breakdown that might otherwise occur, not to mention the really major repair-bill you might also have to pay.

CHAPTER 5

HOW TO SAVE 20 TO 30 PER CENT ON HOME-HEATING BILLS

■ *The major causes of heat loss in a house . . . When insulation, weather stripping, and storm windows can reduce fuel bills and when they cannot . . . Eliminating fuel waste in the furnace . . . Gas versus oil versus electric heat—which is cheaper where you live? . . . Better heating with warm-air, hot-water, and steam heat . . . Best ways to reduce fuel bills and achieve better heating efficiency.*

You COULD heat your house with a candle or at practically no cost at all if it were built like a cold-storage room. That means walls, floor, and roof solidly packed with blocks of insulation so that an absolute minimum of heat can leak out.

In such a house the windows would be built with at least three sheets of glass (triple storm-windows) with an inert air space between the glass layers. The doors would be sealed with refrigeratorlike gaskets. Outside air would be drawn in for ventilation, but it would be heated or cooled (also filtered) before being let in, according to the outdoor air-temperature.

The cost of heating such a house in even the coldest climate would run no more than $25 to $30 a winter, or one tenth of the $250 to $300 cost to heat a typical three-bedroom American house of conventional construction. (That, by the way, makes heating one of the larger home-ownership costs.) That low $25 to $30 figure was not pulled out of the air. It's based on the cost of heating test houses built for research.

The high cost and impracticality of building a house with such fortresslike construction rules it out for most people, but actual houses with very good thermal design for low-cost heating have been built. For example, in Minneapolis, Minnesota, where it

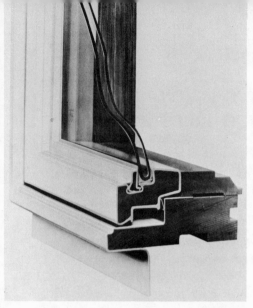

gets down to 40° below zero in winter, a group of three-bedroom houses with some 1,300 square feet of floor area are heated for an average fuel cost of a mere $83 a house per winter. That's for nine months of heating and despite the fact that the houses are of contemporary design with very large glass window-walls. The trick is that the builder, Robert Norsen, who's also an engineer, heavily insulated the walls and roof of the house. Among other things, all the window glass is double-pane insulating glass. A very small amount of the house heat leaks through the structure to outdoors. The houses are remarkably warm and comfortable, and the fuel bills are rock bottom.

Norsen's houses are by no means unique. Other builders, architects, and homeowners, too, are discovering that effectively insulating a house is the number one requisite today for low-cost heating. An additional benefit is the improved comfort that also results. There are fewer cold walls, drafts, and cold spots in the house. Cold walls in a house draw off heat from the body's skin surface faster than the blood can offset the loss of the heat. You feel cold and chilly for the same reason you get goose pimples standing in front of an open refrigerator. In a house with cold walls you may try to compensate by raising the heating thermostat for more heat. That does little good because only the indoor *air* temperature is increased. The cold walls and other cold parts of

This variety of insulating materials includes loose wool that is poured out of a bag (right), a five-foot-long aluminum-foil-covered bat (lower left), and roll insulation (center right). Various building materials that also insulate, such as ceiling tiles (bottom) and insulated paneling (rear), can be specified when you remodel.   BETTER HOMES & GARDENS.

the house shell remain virtually as cold as before. They continue to drain off body heat and contribute to your discomfort.

If, however, the walls, floor, and ceiling are well insulated, these surfaces don't get so cold. Substantially less body heat is lost to the cold surfaces around, and you're kept "warmer." Moreover, the thermostat need not be raised for more heat. A well-insulated house (which in a cold climate calls for storm windows and storm doors, as well as insulation) will be cozy and comfortable at about 70–72° F. A poorly insulated house requires an interior air temperature of 75° or more. That is one of the little-known reasons why insulation reduces fuel bills and saves money. In other words, a lower air temperature, and thus less heat, is required to keep humans comfortable in a well-insulated house than in a house with little or no insulation.

REDUCING HEAT LOSS FROM YOUR HOUSE

Storm windows and doors are particularly important in a cold climate but less necessary, if at all, in the warm South. They will do good on all four sides of a house. Window glass and walls lashed by cold winds are the greatest source of heat loss from a house. If you must economize, at least put them on the exposed north or windward sides of the house. If the prevailing wind in winter where you live comes from the northeast, put them on the north and east; if from the west, put them on the west. You might omit them from the less-cold south side of your house and save their cost. Though the exterior shell of your living space should be well insulated, doing this to an existing house can get expensive. More on this in a moment.

You can usually tell if your house shell requires insulation simply by putting the palm of your hand flat against the inside surfaces of your exterior walls during cold weather. If the wall is cold to the touch, it's losing excessive heat to outdoors. For comparison, put the palm of your hand against an interior wall partition. If it feels considerably warmer to the touch than the exterior walls, the outside walls need insulation. Your house may already have some insulation, but the palm test can indicate where you may need more. Apply the palm test to your ceilings to tell how much heat is being lost upward. Also apply it to the first floor of your house, particularly around the outer perimeter of the house near the exterior walls.

Insulating the ceiling is usually easy and relatively cheap in an existing house. You simply put the insulation down between the attic floor beams right over the top-floor ceiling. This can be a simple do-it-yourself job. If your attic is floored over, the flooring sometimes can be pulled up to allow the insulation in; then the flooring is replaced. At least three to four inches of insulation thickness is recommended at the attic floor—six to eight if you have electric heat or central air-conditioning. If you cannot easily remove existing attic flooring, "loose" insulation can be blown in under the flooring by an insulation contractor. If there are rooms in your attic, their walls and ceilings should be insulated. This also can be done by blowing insulation into otherwise inaccessible spaces.

Insulating the walls of an existing house is usually tougher and more expensive. It is, however, by no means impossible even with brick or stone walls. An insulation contractor blows insulation into the interior of the walls with a special machine. The cost will generally run from about fifteen cents to thirty cents per square foot of wall, or anywhere from about six hundred dollars to twelve hundred dollars, more or less, for a typical house. Is it worth it? Only if you expect to stay in a house for at least five or six years. Then the increased comfort plus the fuel savings that result make it a good investment. If your house is air-conditioned, you will get a double saving as a result of reduced summer cooling bills.

If your house has a basement, the first floor generally does not require insulation. The basement may not get cold enough to require insulating it from the rest of the house. If, however, some parts of your first floor are cold—as determined by the palm test —this can be remedied by stuffing pads of insulation up under the floor (at the basement ceiling) usually at an outside wall location; that's where the most cold comes from.

The palm test also can detect other parts of your house that are particularly cold although all the rest is well insulated and warm. This may be the cause of a cold problem, for example, often encountered in a bedroom that is located over an unheated garage or any other cold living-area that is located next to a cold, unheated space. It's often because insulation was omitted from the separating wall when the house was built. Merely insulating such walls can make a whale of a difference inside the house.

Brick walls are insulated as shown here. The bricks are removed, and insulation is pneumatically blown into the hollow wall-spaces. The bricks are replaced with new mortar. Stone and frame walls are done in the same way.

Weather Stripping

Weather stripping consists of specially made strips of rubber, felt, or plastic which are put around the frames of doors and windows to prevent cold-air leaks. Again use the hand test around the inside frame of exterior doors and windows. You'll quickly locate jets of cold air zipping in from outdoors. Making the culpable door or window fit tight can minimize the leak, but weather stripping usually must be applied to seal off the leak. Various forms of weather stripping are made for different applications. See what's available at a hardware store or lumber yard and choose the kind that's best for your needs.

To sum up: The key word is insulation. Even thick brick or stone walls should be insulated. Remember that storm windows

The weather stripping shown here is specially designed to seal doors. A variety of other metal and nonmetal kinds are also made for both doors and windows.

and doors also insulate. And weather stripping is the way to cut heat losses at leaky doors and windows.

REDUCING FUEL WASTE WITH OIL HEAT

How you can get more heat for your money depends on whether you have oil, gas, or electric heat. We'll start with oil heat, where much fuel is often wasted because of a dirty oil-burner. Oil burners are easily fouled by soot and carbon, the products of oil combustion. The longer a burner operates, the greater the buildup of soot and carbon. The nature of oil heat requires that the burner be cleaned and readjusted at least once a year, preferably in early fall, and sometimes twice a year. An oil burner that is not cleaned and adjusted regularly will waste an increasing quantity of fuel.

The operating efficiency of an oil burner is determined by a "CO_2 test." The carbon dioxide, smoke content, and temperature of the combustion gases going up the chimney are recorded. This is done in a minute or two. The CO_2 content should be at least 10 per cent, the higher the better. The flue-gas temperature should be between 450° and 600° F.—the lower the better. The smoke content should read between 0 and 2, no higher. These readings mean that an oil burner is operating at high efficiency.

If your burner cannot achieve such results, you'll probably do well to replace it. A new oil-burner may cost a few hundred dollars, but you should get this money back in spades in a few years. A whole new heating unit is generally not needed.

When your oil burner is serviced, be sure that the inside of the heating unit (the fire chamber) is also cleaned. Soot and scale should be cleaned out. If necessary, the serviceman should wire-brush the dirt and scale off the inside walls.

"Firebox" Liners

The efficiency of oil heating can be sharply increased if the fire chamber (firebox) contains an aluminum-silicate ceramic-fiber liner. Most oil heaters made since about 1963 contain this kind of liner, but check yours to be sure. If it lacks the liner, get one. An aluminum-silicate liner can increase your combustion efficiency by as much as 25 per cent. It's a material originally developed to shield astronauts from extreme temperatures in space. Inside a heating plant it gives a hotter, more productive fire. One ordinarily can be installed for about twenty-five dollars. One kind of oil heater will not accept such liners; it's a heating unit with a horizontal stainless-steel fire-chamber.

Other Oil-Heat Tips

Use good-grade oil of a brand that contains chemical additives that, among other things, prevent sludge from building up in your oil tank. The best assurance of getting oil with additives is using a well-known brand of oil, and not a cheap, off-brand oil. (It's cheap because it's no good.)

Your serviceman should put a corrosion-resistant chemical in your oil tank at least once every two or three years. It usually comes as a powder or in crystal form. It can prevent the tank from rusting out, which would require a new tank.

Stock up on fuel oil when it's cheap, which means buying in summer or early fall. This can save up to 10 per cent on fuel cost.

IF YOU HAVE GAS HEAT

The carbon-dioxide test used for oil heat will also tell how well a gas heater is operating. A gas heater, however, requires less checking and readjustment than an oil heater, because gas is a cleaner fuel; it leaves less carbon and soot when burned. A gas heater generally needs to be checked, cleaned, and adjusted no more than once every three or four years.

A good heating man can make the test, or you might call the gas company to do it. At the very least, the serviceman should carry out what is called a "clock-the-meter" test. He measures the amount of gas burned in a full minute to determine if the unit is properly adjusted.

The color and appearance of the flame inside the heater will usually tell you whether or not you're getting efficient combustion. The flame should be a clear blue with no more than a touch of yellow or orange. A good serviceman can tell at a glance if it's right. Learn from him how to observe the flame safely and what it should look like, and then you can inspect it periodically yourself.

An occasional cleaning of the gas burner and heater can also help. It reduces the possibility of a misadjustment. Dust, lint, and dirt are less likely to cause trouble.

WARM-AIR HEAT

You may have gas, oil, or electric heat, and it could also be warm-air or hot-water heat. The fuel can vary, in other words, but if the medium by which heat is supplied to the house is air, it's a warm-air system. Air is heated in a furnace and delivered to your rooms through ducts. If water is heated and delivered through pipes to room radiators, it's hot-water heat. If steam is generated and delivered to the radiators, it's a steam system.

If air is heated and merely allowed to rise up to your rooms by virtue of the fact that warm air naturally rises, it's called a gravity warm-air system. Gravity systems are seldom installed in new houses today, but quite a few are still around in old houses. If the heated air is circulated by a blower through the ducts, it's a forced warm-air system, the most common kind of warm-air heat today.

A dirty air-filter is one of the most common causes of poor heating with forced warm-air heat. Dirt and dust removed from the airstream gradually clog up the filter. That's why the filter must periodically be removed and cleaned or replaced. If it is not, it will get so clogged that little heat can get to the house. Eventually the furnace could overheat and crack up, which would call

A thermostat's operation is vital for good heating, and it can also give you information. For example, if you must keep your house at 75° F. or more for comfort, the house is usually not well insulated. The top dial is set for the temperature desired, and the bottom dial indicates room temperature.

for a new furnace. Moral: Pull your filter regularly and vacuum or replace it, depending on the kind you have. Experience will tell you how often it must be cleaned. This could be from every two or three months to up to twice that, depending on the house.

No matter what kind of warm-air heat you have, keep the air grilles free of obstructions. Toys and papers as well as dust will get into them and can obstruct the air circulation.

For top efficiency with forced warm-air heat have your furnace and blower set to operate according to what engineers call Continuous Air Circulation, or CAC for short. If you have poor heating now, this could be the glorious remedy. Researchers have found that switching the system to CAC operation cures more than 90 per cent of all heating problems with forced warm-air heat.

The blower is set so that it operates most or all of the time, regardless of whether the thermostat is calling for heat or not. Air flows through the house continuously. Ordinarily, the blower goes on to circulate air only when the thermostat calls for heat and the furnace burners start up. When the burners cut off, the blower stops, and there is no air flow until the thermostat again calls for heat and turns on the furnace burners. That's intermittent-blower operation. It's actually jerky, on-off operation and is the reason why so many warm-air systems provide jerky, inefficient heating.

Switch your furnace to CAC operation, and all the air in the house is kept gently and continuously in motion. Pockets of cold air are not allowed to settle at floor level. Pockets of warm air cannot stratify at the ceiling. More-uniform heating results throughout the house because of the leveling effect of continuous air-circulation. This means, among other things, that some rooms don't get hot and stuffy and others don't get cold. Research at the University of Illinois showed that temperatures inside a house with old-fashioned, intermittent-blower operation will rise and fall three to four degrees during a full heating cycle. Switched to CAC, the heating system in the same house kept the temperature fluctuating less than one and one-half degrees, which is pretty good.

With CAC operation your electric bill will go up a bit because the blower runs all the time. The increased electricity used will ordinarily cost no more than ten dollars to fifteen dollars a winter, but this extra cost is usually offset by savings on fuel, because of the more efficient heating that results. In addition, CAC operation is better for the blower motor; it will last longer, compared to the greater wear and tear and shorter motor life with jerky, on-off operation.

With CAC operation "cold" air will occasionally seem to come from the air registers, which bothers some people. Actually, the air is no cooler than room temperature. Don't worry about this. If the air causes a slight draft or two, usually a slight rearrangement of furniture will put people out of the way.

How to Switch Your Furnace to CAC

All that you need usually do to change to CAC is flick a switch at the furnace. It's the fan-control switch, which you put on its "continuous" setting. On some systems you change it from "fan" to "automatic" setting. Look for this switch on or near the furnace.

Sometimes it is called a "summer-winter switch"; you set it on the "summer" setting, even in winter.

If you're unsure about the switch, ask your heating dealer. For full benefits from CAC, other adjustments could also be made to the heating system by a serviceman. Discuss this too with your heating dealer. Not all heating men, however, know about CAC. If your serviceman ignores or scorns it, he is clearly years behind the times, and it could be worth your while to switch to a twentieth-century serviceman.

HOT-WATER AND STEAM HEAT

With both hot-water and steam heat it is important not to block the air flow around the radiators. The air should have free movement under and all around a radiator. At least an inch or two of clearance is necessary between any furniture and the radiator.

A bad offender is a radiator cover that prevents the heat from flowing straight up from the radiator. A cover should have vents to let air circulate around the radiator and then up to the room. If a cover or shelf blocks the air from a radiator, drill a series of holes in the top of the cover to let the heat do its job. Be sure that the room air can flow freely to the radiator.

Get more heat from each radiator by placing a sheet of aluminum foil on the wall directly behind the radiator. The foil, which should be the same height and width as the radiator, will bounce radiator heat back into the house, rather than let it leak out through the wall.

Open the drain valve at the base of the heating boiler at least once a year, and let the water run out. Turn the heat off first, of course, and put a pail underneath to catch the water. This will drain off sludge and dirt from inside the boiler water. Refill the boiler to the proper mark on the water scale (steam heat) or altitude gauge (hot-water heat). Mark that gauge level before you drain off water so water can be added to the same level later.

Radiators should heat up uniformly all over. If not, something's wrong. Check the shut-off valve (the hand valve at the pipe inlet to the radiator). It should be open all the way, especially with steam heat. Keeping it partly closed to save heat generally wastes heat. Keep it full open or closed, one or the other.

If the valve is open and the radiator still doesn't heat evenly, check the little valve vent at the opposite end, usually located halfway up the radiator. Its purpose is to let air escape so that hot water or steam can fill the radiator. A hot-water radiator should be "bled" at least once a year, usually in the fall—later, too, if necessary. Use a screwdriver or radiator key to open the valve until water starts to flow. Then close it immediately. Again, hold a pail underneath for safety. A radiator with an automatic self-bleeding vent does not need manual bleeding.

The valve vent on a steam radiator should work automatically, allowing air to escape as steam enters. It closes when the hot steam hits it. Sometimes these vents will clog up, trapping air inside the radiator, and steam cannot enter. If a steam radiator does not heat, unscrew the vent and remove it. If a rush of air and steam pours out, the vent is not working properly. Sometimes it can be cleaned by blowing through it or by boiling it in a caustic solution. As a rule, though, it is best to discard a bad valve and replace it. Use a new adjustable kind that lets you regulate air escape time. Replacing old, nonadjustable vents with the adjustable kind is recommended if your steam heat is sick a lot. The new vents will permit adjustments so that the radiators can heat up at the same rate, no matter how far away from the heater each is. They're not expensive and are sold in most hardware stores.

ELECTRIC HEAT

One of the biggest advantages of electric heat is its gloriously small need for service and maintenance. There's no major boiler or furnace equipment to go wrong. Electric heat can be expensive, though, unless a house is very well insulated and also has storm windows and doors. At least six to eight inches of insulation is recommended at the attic floor, the walls should be full-thick with insulation, and storm windows are recommended on every side of the house. Such complete buttoning-up may not be essential with electric heat in a mild southern climate, especially if you have low electric rates, but it can still help.

Service and maintenance is usually minimal with electric heat. If you have electric baseboard heaters, keep the inside fins clean. Remove the cover of each occasionally and vacuum the inside. Also be sure that, as with radiators, air can circulate freely under and around the baseboards.

Turn the heat down in unoccupied rooms such as bedrooms during the day, other rooms at night. That's assuming, of course, that you have a thermostat in each room, which is often the case with electric heat.

GENERAL HEATING TIPS

Regardless of the kind of heating you have, certain parts of the system may require an occasional drop or two of oil. This and other maintenance should be mentioned in the manufacturer's instruction booklet. Get it out to see how a little loving (or grudging) care once in a while can keep things working smoothly and prevent problems and an expensive repair bill. If you don't have an instruction book, write to the manufacturer for one, telling him the model and serial number on your heater.

Close the fireplace damper when the fireplace is not in use. An open damper lets warm house-air escape up the chimney.

Don't fiddle with the thermostat. Set it at 70–75° F. or wherever you want it, and let it be. It's a common misconception that the higher the thermostat is set, the faster the furnace will heat. The furnace burns at one rate when it's on. A cold house will not heat up to 70° any faster with the thermostat set at 80° than at 70°. An 80° setting can waste a lot of fuel.

The temperature you use, like the company you keep, is a matter of personal preference and need. Obviously, the lower the temperature, the less heat needed and the less fuel burned. Heating costs increase by about 3 per cent for every degree above 70° F.

With gas heat, keep the furnace pilot-light on in summer. It keeps your heating equipment dry during humid summer weather, reducing the possibility of rust and corrosion inside. It can also save the cost of service if you would otherwise need a serviceman in fall to relight the pilot. Nearly everyone, however, should be able to relight his own pilot. It's simple to do and not at all hazardous when properly done.

Be sure your thermostat is properly located. The thermostat should be located on an inside wall out of reach of cold drafts from windows or doors and also away from the heat of a fireplace, radiator, or lamp. Heat or cold from such sources can cause erratic thermostat operation, and thus erratic, wasteful heating.

Thermostat Setback at Night

About 10 to 15 per cent can be saved on overnight fuel consumption by setting your heating thermostat down at bedtime and turning it up again the next morning. The savings, however, depend on several variables; you don't always save.

Set the thermostat down about six or seven degrees, but no more, below its daytime setting: for example, no lower than 65° at night if your daytime setting is 72°. A greater setback does little good, because the heater then has to work overtime the next morning, burning extra fuel, to heat the house up again.

Don't bother with thermostat setback on very cold nights, because little or no savings result then. The savings are greatest when the outdoor temperature at night drops to about 30°. They are less when it is 15° outside and fall off to no fuel conserved on a night of 0° or colder. The colder the night, the more fuel required the next morning to reheat the house—this offsets the nighttime fuel saved.

To make any savings at all, your house must be insulated. The better it's insulated, the greater the night savings. Insulation conserves the heat you start off with in the house when the thermostat is first turned down.

Reviewing thermostat setback: Set your thermostat down no more than six or seven degrees, but only when the nighttime cold does not go below 0° and only if your house is insulated. If it's not insulated, don't bother.

Can You Switch to a Cheaper Fuel?

You can, of course, if you now use oil but gas is cheaper, or vice versa. You may have electric heat, but perhaps gas or oil would be cheaper, possibly substantially so.

It depends on the fuel that is cheapest where you live. As noted in Chapter 2, gas and electric rates in particular vary considerably from city to city and state to state. The price of fuel oil, however, does not fluctuate as much.

Gas will cost as little as 5¢ per therm (one hundred cubic feet usually) in the South and parts of the Midwest, where natural gas is cheap, up to two to three times that price in the Northeast and particularly in New England. As a rule, gas will beat out oil for heating economy if natural gas costs you no more than about 14¢ per therm. That's compared with paying 18¢ per gallon for fuel oil. In other words if natural gas costs you 14¢ per therm or less, it will usually pay you to switch from oil to gas. If you already have gas heat, stay with it.

The lower the price of gas below 14¢, the greater your savings will be, compared with heating with 18¢ oil. If you pay more than 18¢ a gallon for oil, you therefore save by paying a little more for gas. For example, if you pay 10 per cent more than that for oil, gas will be cheaper for house heating at up to 15.4¢ per therm

(10 per cent higher than 14¢ gas). Conversely, if gas costs more than 14¢ a therm, heating with 18¢ oil is generally cheaper; the higher the cost of gas over 14¢, the proportionately more you can spend for oil. The price you pay for gas can be determined from your winter gas bills, as explained in Chapter 2, or by a call to the gas company. Frankly ask an engineer there whether gas is cheaper than oil heat. The man will often give you an honest answer, but if he hems and haws and tries to sell you on gas for reasons other than economy, the chances are that gas heat is not economical.

Electric-Heat Cost

As a general rule electricity must be very cheap to cost less to heat your house than gas or oil. Ordinarily, it should cost no more than about 1¢ per kilowatt hour (kw. hr.) to be competitive with gas at about 14¢ per therm or oil at 18¢ per gallon. If electricity costs more than 1¢, it will generally mean higher heating bills. That makes electric heat really economical only in a low-cost power area, such as the T.V.A. region and the Pacific Northwest.

A growing number of electric untility companies in other parts of the country, however, are lowering their rates for electric heat. As a result, electric heat is growing in popularity. Even at 1.5¢ per kw. hr., in a new house properly built and insulated, electric heat can have major advantages, costing you little or no more than gas or oil heat. This is partly because the special low electric rate you get for electric heat can also mean savings on other electricity used in your house.

By and large, however, it does not pay to switch an existing house from gas or oil to electric heat. It generally will pay only if the whole house is being renovated and thoroughly insulated.

Electric heat can, however, be a strong contender for heating a new room or other new space added to an existing house. It often offers savings on installation price, compared with extending an existing hot-water or warm-air heating system to the living space.

As noted in Chapter 2, your bill for electricity, including electric heat for a new room or two added to your house, could also be reduced if you have an electric water-heater and you get a cut-price break on the total cost of all your electricity.

Summed up, getting good heating for the least money is done in two ways, and both should be exploited. First, concentrate on making your house tight and well insulated to cut down excessive loss of house heat through walls and glass to the cold outdoors. Second, get the most out of your heating system and maximum heating effect from every unit of fuel energy burned. That includes using the fuel that is cheapest where you live.

CHAPTER 6   LOW-COST HOME
AIR-CONDITIONING

*Reducing air-conditioning bills by reducing the chief sources
of heat in houses . . . How to operate air conditioning—room
coolers and central systems—at top efficiency . . . Causes of
high house humidity and how to eliminate them . . . Ways to
get a small cooler to do a big job during a heat wave . . .
Typical problems with home air-conditioning and what to do
about them . . . How to buy central air-conditioning . . .
Choosing a good dealer and reducing the purchase price . . .
Air-cooled versus water-cooled equipment . . . Electric versus
gas air-conditioning . . . Buying a room air-conditioner . . . How
to tell a good-quality unit.*

HERE ARE the things to know if you already have an air-conditioned house or if you are considering air conditioning.

A house of up to 1,250 square feet of area—a 25-by-40-foot ranch house, for example—can be totally air-conditioned for about $50 a summer in the North or up to $100 a summer for five and a half months of cooling in the hot South. Houses of up to 1,750 square feet can be centrally air-conditioned for $65 to $75 a summer in the North and $140 to $150 in the South.

Those figures are a matter of record for insulated houses, based on an electrical cost of 2¢ per kilowatt hour, which is about the average cost for household electricity in the United States. Thus your operating costs for central air-conditioning should be about $4 per 100 square feet of house in the North up to $8 in hot parts of the South, such as Texas and Arizona.

It will be a little more or less depending on whether you pay more or less than 2¢ per kilowatt hour for electricity. It also depends on such things as how you operate your air conditioning.

Typical Operating Costs for Central Air-Conditioning

	Normal Summer High Temperature	Approx. Elec. Rate for Cooling per Kw. Hr.	Approx. Hours of Operation per Summer	Approx. Operating Cost per Ton of Cooling Capacity	Average Total Operating Cost for Typical 1,200 Sq. Ft. House
Akron, Ohio	95°	1.85¢	600	$18	$36
Atlanta, Ga.	95	1.60	1500	28	56
Baltimore, Md.	95	1.75	800	25	50
Boston, Mass.	92	3.10	250–400	12.50–13	25
Charlotte, N.C.	95	2.00	1000	32	62
Chicago, Ill.	95	2.50	500	18	36
Cleveland, Ohio	95	2.00	350	15	30
Corpus Christi, Texas	95	2.00	3500	53	100
Dallas, Texas	100	1.86¢	1400	41	82
Denver, Colo.	95	2.10	600	25	50
Detroit, Mich.	95	2.00	500	12	24
Ft. Worth, Texas	100	2.00	1400	50	100
Hartford, Conn.	93	2.50	500–650	26	52
Houston, Texas	95	1.50	1000	42.50	85
Indianapolis, Ind.	95	2.00	1500	25–30	60
Kansas City, Mo.	100	2.50	900	33	66
Long Island, N.Y.	95	2.00	750	25	50
Los Angeles, Calif.	90	1.40	800	25	50
Madison, Wis.	95	2.30	300	21	42
Montgomery, Ala.	95	1.30	1300	30–35	64
Newark, N.J.	95	2.05	500	20–25	45
New Haven, Conn.	95	2.00	750	15	30
New Orleans, La.	95	1.50	1800	60–65	125
New York, N.Y.	95	3.10	500	20	40
Oklahoma City Okla.	101	2.10	1000	32	64
Philadelphia, Pa.	95	1.81	800	20	40
Portland, Ore.	90	1.10	250	3	7–10
Raleigh, N.C.	95	1.50	1100	35	65
Richmond, Va.	95	1.5–1.8	1000	25	50
Rochester, N.Y.	95	1.80	400	12.50	25
Salt Lake City, Utah	95	1.55	750	12	23
San Francisco, Calif.	85	1.28	1000	30	60
Shreveport, La.	100	2.00	2400	48	96
Springfield, Ill.	98	2.00	700	20	40.50
St. Louis, Mo.	95	2.00	1000	23	56
Tampa, Fla.	95	1.50	1750	30	60
Tucson, Ariz.	105	1.65	2200	65	125
Washington, D.C.	95	1.80	1000	20–25	50–60

Nearly anybody can do certain things to get more air-conditioning per dollar expended. Certain human mistakes are often made with air conditioning which cause both operating bills and the interior temperature and humidity in houses to climb to uncomfortably high levels. It's easy to avoid them.

How much do you pay for air conditioning? If it's more than $4 to $8 per 100 square feet of air-conditioned living area, you're doing something wrong. If that's all you pay, you could probably reduce the bill. If you don't have air conditioning, you can benefit by knowing how to reduce the cost and therefore get a good system at the lowest cost. The number one rule to remember is that the more you can reduce the summer heat load inside of your house, the less air-conditioning needed, and thus the lower the cost. A second rule has to do with knowing about the proper care and feeding of an air-conditioning system. Like a puppy dog, it requires a little coddling and attention to thrive. You don't have to be a mechanical genius or even know how to operate a screwdriver to make the cooling equipment perform well.

IF YOU DO NOT HAVE AIR CONDITIONING

"It doesn't get that hot where we live, so why get it?" Famous last words (and the family may suffer miserably when the heat of July and August arrives).

"It's not the heat, it's the humidity." It's actually both; usually it's a combination of the two that makes things oppressive. Air conditioning neutralizes both, wringing soggy moisture from the air as well as lowering the temperature.

The figures in the table are actual costs, gathered from air-conditioning engineers and electric companies in each city, adjusted for a 1,200-square-foot house (a 30-by-40-foot ranch house, for example). Costs for larger houses would be proportionately higher; thus the operating cost for a house twice as large would be twice the figure in the table for the city given. Note that the outdoor temperature can get as hot in the North as in the South, though costs are higher in the South because summers are longer.

These two houses, located in Texas, illustrate excellent design for air conditioning. As a result both are completely air-conditioned from April to October for less than one hundred dollars a summer, despite 100°-plus weather. Wide roof overhangs shade the window glass from the sun. The carport of the white house was put on the west side of the house to shade the house from the afternoon sun. Similar design measures may not lend themselves to an existing house, but the principles still apply and can often be realized in other ways.

"It's too expensive." That's another objection that is quite valid for people who just don't have the money, but air conditioning today does cost less than many people think. It can be economically justified just in terms of its health and living benefits: You can sleep all night when a heat wave strikes, and you will be healthier and work better. It's a particular boon to the health and survival of people with allergies and heart conditions. Doctors prescribe it as medicine for these and other ailments that are aggravated by heat. A family sleeps and eats better in an air-conditioned house. There are few summer colds, despite widespread belief to the contrary. Tempers don't flare up, because everybody's disposition is cooled off along with the air in the house.

An air-conditioned house is also easier to keep clean than a non-air-conditioned house with all its windows flung wide open to dirt and soot from outdoors. Salt shakers flow all summer long, and mildew and dankness problems are eliminated.

Those are some of the reasons why more than six million families had central air-conditioning in their houses at the beginning of the 1970's. Central air-conditioning systems were being installed in new and old houses at a rate of more than one million a year by 1970. Another fifteen to twenty million families had one or more room coolers in their homes or apartments.

Air conditioning is clearly becoming a standard part of houses. In fact, a house without it in the $25,000-and-up price range is hard to sell in many parts of the South today. Within a few years air conditioning is expected to become an equally strong sales feature, or no-sale feature if you don't have it, in the North. In short, air conditioning also represents an excellent investment, and its cost should come back to you via an increased sales price when you sell your house.

IF YOU ALREADY HAVE AIR CONDITIONING

Your air conditioning may be a room cooler or a central system. Remember that the more you cut down the entry of hot outdoor heat and reduce the buildup of interior heat, the less load there is on the air-conditioner. The equipment won't have to work as hard and will use less power, so your operating bills will go down. Here are effective ways to do that and get the most out of your equipment.

1. Don't let hot sun pour into your house, especially through windows. Shade the glass, pull blinds down on the inside, or put up blinds on the outside. An enormous quantity of heat is unleashed into a house by direct sun shining through windows. That's why greenhouse temperatures climb to ovenlike levels.

What's more, the sun pours as much heat per hour per square foot of glass exposure into a house from the east in the morning as it does from the west in the afternoon. The sun may not seem as hot in the morning, because the air temperature is not as hot as in the afternoon. Nonetheless, morning sun will drain overnight coolness from a house and start your interior heat load building up early. That makes the house tougher to keep cool later when the daytime heat level reaches its peak.

Shading a window on the outside is about twice as effective as interior shading. Sometimes a retractable drop-shade on the outside can do the trick, or consider the use of awnings, especially if you live in a very hot climate. Such add-on measures should, of course, be architecturally suitable for your house.

2. Stop roof-heat entry. Sun pouring down on the roof is the single biggest source of summer heat in most houses and accounts for the biggest portion of air-conditioning bills. That's because the sun beats down on the roof virtually all day long, but only on a single wall or window exposure at any one time during the day. Attics get as hot as 150° F., and this furnacelike heat seeps down into the house long into the evening. That's why upstairs rooms are generally hotter than first-floor rooms.

The best protection from attic heat is a thick layer of six to eight inches of insulation at the attic floor. At the same time the attic should be well ventilated. This calls for large screened air-vents in the attic to let outside air blow in and wash out the hot air.

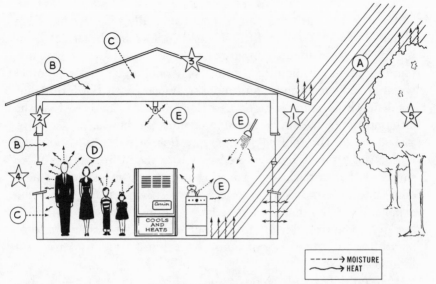

Chief sources of heat and thus air-conditioning expense in a house are: (A) hot sunshine; (B) outside-air heat; (C) water vapor (humidity) from outside air; (D) human heat and moisture; (E) heat and moisture generated inside the house. The first two may account for as much as 75 per cent of the total heat load and thus three quarters of your air-conditioning bill. That's why it's important to shade windows from the sun, insulate the house structure, and ventilate the attic. CARRIER CORPORATION.

A really hot attic with little or no insulation can be cooled effectively by an attic ventilating-fan. It can do wonders to reduce your cooling bills. The fan is set up to blow hot air out one end of the attic, and cooler outdoor replacement air is automatically drawn in through a vent at the other end. A continuous air-wash results, which can substantially reduce the attic heat. A small thermostat, wired to the fan, can automatically turn it on when the attic temperature climbs above, say, 90°, and turn the fan off when the attic temperature falls below 90°.

A regular window fan, designed for installation in a window, can be used. It should be large enough to provide one complete air change through the attic at least every five minutes (every three minutes for good results in a very hot climate).

An attic heat-leveling fan can be especially effective in a hot climate, where you need little or no attic-floor insulation for heating purposes, and also in a house where the air-conditioning equipment has difficulty keeping you cool during hot summer weather. It is used more and more in houses with borderline air-conditioning systems—it reduces the total heat-load, so that the air-conditioner has an easier time cooling the house.

The darker the roof color, the more heat it will absorb and the hotter the attic. A light-colored or white roof thus reflects more sun heat than a dark roof. Painting a roof white just to cut heat entry and air-conditioning costs, however, is often not worth the expense; it will generally not reduce attic heat by that much. If, however, you are getting a new roof or building a new house or an addition to your present house, you might want to consider a light-colored roof.

3. Keep doors and windows shut. This should be obvious, but servicemen find that a surprising number of people have air-conditioning problems—and high cooling bills—because windows and doors are blithely left wide open while the equipment is running. Hot outdoor air blows in and expensive cool air blows out.

A window or two can be left open a little and not make much difference in cooling operation. This is perfectly all right and understandable in, say, a bedroom where one desires "fresh" air all night long. If a child leaves a door open occasionally, this too should not be a cause of alarm, and there's really no need to scream at the child. If children chronically leave a door flung open, an automatic door-closer will reduce the loss of cool air.

4. Leave storm windows on in summer. Don't take them all down and put on your screens, since windows are infrequently opened in a room or house with air conditioning. A few storm windows can be replaced with screens, if desired, to let you enjoy the breeze on mild summer days. Storm windows left on in summer also give a double-glass shield that cuts down on outside air heat entry into a house through your window glass. Storm windows, however, do not reduce direct sun heat entry through glass by very much.

5. Make sure the clothes dryer is vented. A clothes dryer can spew out a huge exhaust of hot, wet air even when it's located in the basement. The hot vapor infiltrates the living quarters and puts an extra load on the air-conditioner. Vent your dryer!

6. Don't let moisture build up inside the house. Water vapor from cooking, washing, and even a wet basement can, like the vapor from a clothes dryer, sharply increase the humidity in a house and thus make an air-conditioner work harder. In addition to cooling your air, remember that an air-conditioner also wrings moisture from the house air; it dehumidifies.

Steaming cooking vapors and fumes are best eliminated by a kitchen exhaust-fan (preferably located in the outer wall or ceiling directly over the range). Use the fan during cooking. Replacement air from outdoors should be drawn in by opening a kitchen window a few inches rather than by drawing cool air from the rest of the house.

House chores that create moisture, such as washing floors and windows and ironing (especially with a steam iron) can be done early in the day. If you can avoid it, don't hang wet clothes to dry inside the house. This moisture released into the house air requires extra work by the air-conditioner.

A wet cellar should be dried out, since much of the vapor downstairs will inexorably rise upstairs. A slightly damp cellar that cannot be effectively dried out can, on the other hand, be kept dry by spilling a little air-conditioned air into the basement. This may require a cooling outlet installed in the basement. Among other things, this will prevent cellar mildew and wood rot.

Use plastic shower-curtains in bathrooms. Canvas and cloth ones absorb shower water, which later evaporates into the house air and loads down the air-conditioner. A small bathroom exhaust-fan, though not always essential, can also help you rid your house of the clouds of bathroom vapor after a shower or bath. It can be worthwhile with a large family that takes frequent showers.

7. Consider insulating the house walls. This assumes that they're not insulated now. Insulation is particularly recommended for the walls of a large house with considerable wall area or if your walls are exposed to a lot of hot sunshine. An

investment in wall insulation for an existing house generally will pay only if you remain in the house for about five years, as we noted earlier.

8. Turn on the main electric-switch for central air-conditioning equipment before the beginning of summer and at least a day or two before a need for air conditioning is anticipated. This is to warm up the internal cockles of the equipment in advance of operation. It's done by a small electric coil inside the equipment (but there are some brands that don't have this—check yours). The air-conditioner will loosen up and be ready to run efficiently when it is first turned on. You avoid excessive wear that might otherwise occur when starting up from scratch.

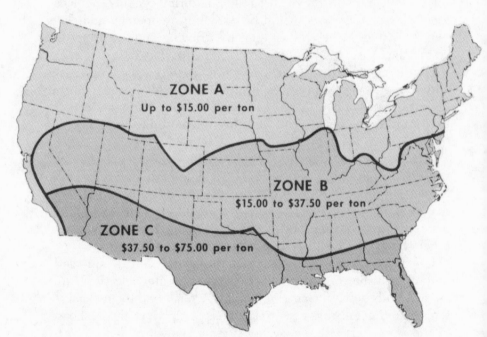

Operating costs for central air-conditioning vary according to the climate zone as well as the cooling capacity required for a house. These figures are based on an electricity cost of 1.5¢ per kilowatt hour. The better your house is shaded and insulated from outdoor sun and heat, the lower the cost, especially in Zones A and B. CARRIER CORPORATION.

9. Don't turn the air-conditioner on and off. Don't keep it off in the morning, say, when it seems cool or when you leave the house unoccupied and then switch it back on later when you return. Don't turn it off at night and fling open your windows before going to bed.

You'll get better results and lower bills if you let the thermostat control operate at all times or nearly so. Set it at 75° F., more or less, and let the cooler go on and off as needed. If you turn it off and later turn it on when things are getting hot, the equipment has to work overtime to get rid of all the house heat and humidity that built up when it was off. Turning off the equipment when things may seem cool will ordinarily gain you little or nothing.

Of course, if the weather turns beautifully cool and comfortable for a few days or a week or so, it's perfectly all right to fling open a few windows and enjoy the breeze. Then turn the equipment off for a while, or better still, set the thermostat up to about 80°. The system will not go on unless there is a pronounced rise in the house temperature. Opening windows is not recommended, of course, if it is important to keep your house air free of pollen to protect an allergic person in your family.

If you leave the house empty for two or three days, it's still good to leave the cooling on. Set the thermostat a little higher than normally, at about 80° or so, to keep things reasonably cool. Then on your return the air-conditioner has only a little way to go to get the house down to a comfortable 75°. If you turn the system off when you leave for a few days, your house could be broiling on your return. It can take a half a day or so before the air-conditioner gets the house cool again. If you'll be away for more than a few days, turn the cooling system off. Your house will probably be hot when you return, but you can obviate this too by having a neighbor turn the cooling on a day or so before you plan to return.

10. Take advantage of "storage effect." During a heat wave lower the thermostat setting three or four degrees below normal before going to bed at night. This is the other exception to the no-fiddling-with-the-thermostat rule. Turn the thermostat down

to at least 72° F. Your house is cooled more than usual while you sleep. Everything in the house—furniture and furnishings as well as ten to twenty tons of structure—will be gradually cooled down at a time when the equipment need not work hard. In effect, extra cooling is stored up to fight off the scorching heat of the next day. When the temperature soars the next day, you will be inexpensively cool because of "storage effect." The cooled-down house and all its cooled-down contents help the air-conditioner fight off the big heat of the day.

Storing up cooling can also help before a party or at any other time when people are expected. People make heat, particularly when they smoke. The additional "people load" from a gathering can make things uncomfortably warm even in an air-conditioned house. You prevent it by cooling down the house ahead of time and letting storage effect help keep things comfortable.

11. Let the cooling blower run all the time. This utilizes the for warm-air heating in winter. The air blower runs all the time, same principle, Continuous Air Circulation (CAC), recommended circulating air continuously through the house when the cooling compressor is off as well as when it's on. The small extra cost to keep the blower running is offset by the money saved as a result of greater air-conditioning efficiency. It also means greater comfort and more uniform temperature control.

The air-conditioning blower, often the same blower used for heating, can generally be turned to continuous operation with the "summer-winter switch" usually located on the equipment. You may also have to set your thermostat to "continuous operation." Call your air-conditioning dealer and ask how to do it.

11. Keep the air filter clean. It is as important for cooling as it is for heating, and it's usually the same filter. Check it at the beginning of summer and clean or replace it if necessary.

Getting the Most from a Room Air-conditioner

Most of the suggestions just given for central air-conditioning also apply to room coolers, with a few obvious exceptions. A bedroom cooler, for example, need not run all day long when the room is unoccupied. It will help, though, if the thermostat is left no higher than 80–85° F. during the day so that the room does not get furnace-hot. During torrid weather the unit probably will have to be turned on at least an hour or two before bedtime if you want to be cool on retiring.

Air-conditioned rooms should be isolated from non-air-conditioned portions of the house by closed doors. If you have warm-air heat and a room cooler or two, close off the heating outlets in the air-conditioned areas during the summer, particularly the return-air outlets (usually in the floor). This prevents cool air from the room escaping down the ducts.

Common Air-Conditioning Problems in Houses

Here are the most common problems encountered with central air-conditioning systems in houses and what to do about them. Various points mentioned earlier will be repeated, partly to emphasize their importance and partly to give the reader a concise guide to air-conditioning problems.

Not enough cooling, especially on the hottest days. The system is either undersized, not working properly, or you're not operating it properly. Is the air filter clean? Are the cool-air supply registers open? Are large windows exposed to direct sunshine? If so, draw blinds or shades over them when the sun hits. Are you letting the thermostat run the equipment? If not, set the thermostat at 75° or wherever you need it and let it run day and night. Don't turn it off at night and open the windows. During a heat wave turn the thermostat down at night—to 72° or lower—and store up cooling in the house for the next day's onslaught of heat. In fact, try leaving the thermostat at a low 72° or so during the whole heat wave. Your house air may go up to 75° or more part of the time, but that's to be expected during the worst heat.

If none of that helps, direct your attention to the attic. Adding up to six or eight inches of insulation at the attic floor might help, or install a thermostatically operated exhaust-fan in the attic to ventilate it. Remember, this kind of attic fan ventilates the attic only and not the rest of the house.

Uneven cooling. Some parts of the house are too cool, whereas others are too warm. Switch your air-conditioning blower to continuous circulation. You want the air to circulate all the time.

Too much house humidity. The air temperature is low enough, but you still feel sweaty and uncomfortable. It's usually because the equipment is cooling the air but not removing enough water vapor from it; i.e., the relative humidity in the house is not reduced enough. Too much water vapor may be present. It may be from an unvented clothes dryer, a wet basement, fabric shower-curtains, and sometimes from indoor plants that are watered too often. (The water evaporates into the air through the leaves.) Find the water problem and eliminate it.

Too large a unit. Your air-conditioning system may be too large for your house! An oversized unit will quickly cool down a house and then stop working for a while. It runs less frequently than a properly sized unit. As a result, the humidity builds up in a house faster than the heat does during those long off-cycles. The tip-off to this problem: Your air conditioning keeps you coolest and most comfortable on the hottest days of summer. It runs the most then and maintains better control over your house humidity. Things are less comfortable and more sweaty for you during ordinary warm weather, when, say, the outside temperature is between 80° and 90°.

Unfortunately, there may be no easy solution for this problem because it's due to an installation mistake. Your air-conditioning dealer might perhaps trade you a smaller compressor for your oversized one. Or try keeping your house at a lower thermostat temperature to keep the equipment cooling longer. Lower it enough, and your problem will be solved. Your house may begin to feel like an icebox, unfortunately, but you can take some of the chill off by opening a window or two to let a little offsetting heat in. Extra operating cost is the price you pay in this case to achieve good dehumidification.

High cooling bills. Something may be wrong with the equipment, or it may merely need readjustment. A serviceman should check out the system.

Your house may have a very high heat load, and the unit must work overtime to keep you cool. Reduce the heat load, and the cooler can take it a bit easier. Shade those windows from the sun, add insulation to the attic, or, better still, install a fan to cool the attic. You want to get rid of excess moisture and other possible sources of excess heat in the house, as we've already noted.

Noisy operation. This is another irritating problem that, alas, also stems from a poor installation, poor system design, or just plain mediocre equipment that is noisy. With a poor installation the equipment often rattles and vibrates because it is not cushioned to prevent vibration. Metal ducts bang and vibrate because they're attached directly to the blower unit (instead of being connected with a canvas collar). The air whistles loudly through the ducts because the ducts are too small; this sometimes can be lessened if the ducts are lined with acoustical padding to sop up the noise. The first two problems require quieting the equipment with a vibration-free mounting or separating metal ducts from direct connection to the metal blower unit. You will probably need a serviceman for both of these.

If your outside compressor section is too noisy, especially for your neighbors, put a fence up between the equipment

The outdoor section of a house air-conditioning system should be located close to the indoor section in order to keep down the installation cost. It's equally important to locate the outdoor section well away from an outdoor porch or patio to minimize noise. Shrubbery will camouflage the equipment. CARRIER CORPORATION.

and the neighbors who complain. Make it a decorative fence of solid wood or, even better, concrete blocks. Put it close to the compressor to ward off the noise waves.

Poor Room-Cooler Performance

The most common troubles with room coolers are caused by dirt-clogged air filters or coolers too small for the space. The first is easily remedied simply by periodically cleaning or replacing the filter. The second may or may not be correctable. Try reducing the heat load in the room by the methods just suggested for cutting the house heat-load with a central system; i.e., keep doors closed, shade windows, insulate the exterior walls of the room, and if there's an attic above, insulate the ceiling or ventilate the attic. If nothing helps, you may just have to get a larger unit.

BUYING NEW AIR-CONDITIONING: ROOM COOLERS VERSUS A CENTRAL SYSTEM

A central system will almost always cool a whole house better than individual room-coolers will. Its operating cost will also

Heavier insulation is recommended for air conditioning, compared with that needed for heating. At least six inches of mineral-wool insulation is recommended at the ceiling under the attic or roof, as shown here. If the attic is well ventilated and cooled with a fan, such heavy insulation may not be needed. OWENS-CORNING FIBERGLAS.

be lower. If you now have warm-air heat, its installation cost generally will be less than that for room coolers.

If you have warm-air heat, a central system can usually be installed in tandem with the heating system, with your existing ducts being used for circulating cool air in summer. Little or no new ductwork is usually needed. Thus the installation price can be lower than the cost of installing new room-coolers for the whole house.

A two- to three-ton central air-conditioning system can be added to a house with forced warm-air heat for from about $850 up to $1,450, based on 1970 prices. The exact price you pay depends on the amount of labor required to connect the new cooling to your heating system and such things as whether or not your house needs larger electric capacity for the cooling. The price of a large system goes up by about $400 to $500 per additional ton of central cooling needed.

A two- to three-ton air-conditioning system is ordinarily needed to cool a house of from 1,000 to 1,750 square feet of living area. An insulated house ordinarily requires about one ton of air conditioning for every 500 to 600 square feet of living area. A very well insulated house with its large windows shaded from the sun can be cooled by about one ton for every 600 to 700 square feet. Conversely, the hotter your climate, the greater the cooling capacity needed per 100 square feet of house.

One ton of air conditioning, by the way, is not a pile of equipment 2,000 pounds in weight. It's a quantity of cooling capacity equal to the cooling effect you would get if you stood next to a one-ton block of ice. Scientifically, it's the removal of twelve thousand B.t.u.'s of heat from the air every hour. Thus a two-ton unit will remove twenty-four thousand B.t.u.'s of heat an hour.

Back to the central system versus room coolers. If you have hot water, steam, electric heat, or any other kind of heat without air ducts, a central system will generally cost more than room units because new ducts are needed to distribute the cool air. (If you have a one-story house, the new ductwork can often be installed in the attic, dropping cool air through the ceiling to each room, or in the basement, discharging cool air through the floor up into each room.) The cost of the ductwork must be added to the price of the equipment. The total price for a two- to three-ton system will run about $1,500 to $2,500.

A two-story or split-level house requires more ductwork because of the need to get the cool air from floor to floor. The total price for the same new system generally will range from about $1,750 to $3,000—more for larger houses. If you can afford it, a central system will be more satisfactory over the years than room coolers would be. Moreover, one central unit will cost less to operate, maintain, and service than a number of individual room-coolers around the house. If the price is a distinct barrier, room coolers at a lower cost can sometimes be strategically located in those parts of the house primarily in need of cooling.

A common mistake to avoid is the piecemeal installation of home air-conditioning. An Illinois family we know, for example, first tried air-conditioning their house with three room-coolers. They weren't enough. The family added still another unit, and that was not enough. They wanted full-house air-conditioning. They ended up tossing out their room coolers and installing a central air-conditioning system. They also found, by the way, that individual room-coolers can be expensive because new heavy-duty electric circuits are generally required where each unit is installed.

Which kind of air conditioning is right for your house—room coolers or a central system? If you really want to be cool in summer and can afford it, air-condition the whole house. Don't spend money on room coolers and then discover that you really want full-house air-conditioning. If you're still unsure, try a single air-conditioner in a bedroom, for example, and see how you like it. If you want more, step up to a central system then.

How to Buy Central Air-Conditioning

Buy only from a really good, well-established dealer. Before you buy, reduce the heat load in your house to a minimum. Those are the two prime rules to remember.

It's best to buy from a dealer who handles a well-known national brand like Carrier, Lennox, York (a division of Borg-Warner), and sometimes General Electric and Westinghouse. By and large, such dealers tend to have the most experience with home cooling. Get bids from two or three different dealers. Ask each dealer for the names of people whose houses he has air-conditioned. Call some of these people to find out how the jobs turned out. Don't necessarily choose the lowest-price job; that can be folly. One doctor we know got three bids for air conditioning his house: $1,660, $1,840, and $1,930. On checking, he found that the low man had omitted important items that the others had included. He would have been stuck later. He took the middle bid ($1,850) chiefly because it was made by the most experienced dealer around. Among other things, this dealer gave him a list of over 150 homeowners whose houses he had air-conditioned. There's a postscript to that story. Two months later the doctor learned that the dealer who made the low bid and the manufacturer who made his equipment had both gone out of the air-conditioning business.

This is the time to consider insulating your whole house, if necessary, or at least the attic. The attic may already be insulated, but will heavier insulation reduce the air-conditioning load? Ask dealers when they come to survey your house for cooling. Tell them, by the way, to figure on your storm windows being left on in summer. The dealer's survey consists, in effect, of adding up all sources of heat load in your house to determine the total amount of air conditioning needed.

What are the largest heat sources for your house? What can you do to reduce them, if anything? Discuss this with the dealer. If a large expanse of window glass exposed to sun accounts for a lot of heat entry, put a shading device over the glass, and sometimes the next size smaller air-conditioner will cool you.

The author of this book did just that in the house his family air-conditioned. We added insulation, left the storm windows on in summer, and did a few other things, and the total air-conditioning load was reduced to under thirty thousand B.t.u.'s; we needed less than two and a half tons of air conditioning, whereas the dealer had originally figured that a three-ton system was needed. Those measures reduced the cost of the total job by about three hundred dollars. It was not all clear savings; some of that money went for extra insulation. Nonetheless, further savings came in dividends from reduced heating as well as reduced cooling operating costs.

Don't Buy an Oversized Unit

Some dealers will, for example, recommend a four-ton air-conditioning system when a three-ton job would be just as good. This happens because—so the dealers say—many homeowners want enough air conditioning to cool their houses quickly during a heat wave. The dealers claim that many people tend to use their air conditioning only during very hot weather and turn off the system at other times. Extra cooling capacity is therefore needed to cool their houses at such times. If that extra capacity isn't there, the people call the dealer and howl. To forestall such howls, the dealer then begins to sell everybody oversized equipment. If, however, you let your air conditioning run all the time, as described earlier, a smaller-capacity unit will keep you cool and properly dehumidified all the time.

Air-Cooled Equipment

Most air conditioning for houses is air-cooled. The heat extracted from the house is dissipated into the outdoor air. Put another way, outdoor air is pulled through a cooling-coil arrangement to carry off the heat removed from your house air.

The other way to dissipate heat is via water cooling. A stream of water is continually run over the hot refrigerant coil to drain off its heat and carry it off, but considerable quantities of water are usually required, which makes cooling with ordinary city water very expensive. Air-cooled equipment costs more to install, but it reduces operating costs substantially, compared with water cooling. An exception is if you have a large quantity of water available at a low price. It could be a fresh-water stream going by your house, but not a water well unless it has limitless access to an underground supply of water.

Conclusion: If you have a really good and ample source of low-cost water, use it for air conditioning. A good air-conditioning dealer can tell you how much water you need and whether or not it makes sense for your house. If it does, your air conditioning will cost less than with air-cooled equipment.

GAS VERSUS ELECTRIC AIR-CONDITIONING

The great majority of air-conditioning systems are powered by electricity. Like a refrigerator, the cooling compressor, the heart of the system, is driven by electric power. Also like refrigerators, the cooling system can be energized by gas, and gas air-conditioners are growing in popularity.

Gas equipment, however, generally has a greater initial cost than electric air-conditioning. Gas will pay only if cheap natural gas is plentifully available where you live, which means mainly in the Midwest, South, and Southwest. Then the cost of gas operation sometimes can beat out electric cooling by enough to make gas more economical for your house.

This also depends on the comparative cost of gas versus electricity. This varies from community to community. To determine if gas would be cheaper, get operating-cost estimates for both gas and electric air-conditioning. Ask the local gas and electric companies. Buy gas cooling, however, only if the local gas company actively promotes it for home cooling, provides good service, and then only if they have at least several years of experience with gas home air-conditioning on their lines. Otherwise, stick with electric air-conditioning.

BUYING A ROOM AIR-CONDITIONER

Again, buy only from a reputable dealer, one who can guarantee service when you need it. Get a well-made brand. That's obvious advice, of course, but often it's forgotten at the moment of purchase, when many a person switches to what seems like a low-priced bargain. Often, it's low in price because it's low in design and construction quality.

The unit should be large enough to cool the room it's for—more obvious advice, but again, many buyers are tempted to squeeze by with a small cooler to save a few bucks. Later they sweat in an uncomfortably hot room because the cooler, though giving its all, simply isn't big enough to cope with the heat inflicted upon it.

The cooling capacity needed for a room can be easily computed from a form available at dealers. You can also get the form by writing to the Association of Home Appliance Manufacturers, 20 North Wacker Drive, Chicago, Illinois 60606. Ask for room-cooler form CM-1.

To be sure you get the right size cooler, take a sketch or plan of the room to be air-conditioned to the dealer. The plan should show the room dimensions, size and location of doors and windows, whether the walls and ceiling are insulated, ceiling height, the exposure of the room (put in an arrow showing north), what the adjoining rooms are, and also what's upstairs as well as downstairs. With that information a good salesman can figure out the proper size for you in a few minutes.

Judging Room-Cooler Quality

The best-quality unit has the highest efficiency rating in B.t.u.'s per watt. You can check this yourself. A room unit with a cooling capacity of 10,000 B.t.u.'s, for example, has an electrical rating of 1,200 watts. It draws that much electricity. It has a rating of 8.33 B.t.u.'s per watt (10,000 divided by 1,200). The nameplate on the air-conditioner will ordinarily tell you its B.t.u. output and its input in watts of electricity. The very best and highest quality models will have a rating of about 10 B.t.u.'s per watt; the very lowest and poorest ones, about 5 or so.

Don't necessarily buy a room cooler according to brand name.

Some big-name companies make different models of varying quality, the lowest-cost ones being cheaply made. On the other hand, high price doesn't always mean high quality. Sometimes a high price merely means that you pay more for a highly decorative front or a flashy feature or two, which has little effect on operating performance.

You obviously must pay more, though not necessarily top price, for a high-quality unit, but it will operate more efficiently and thus lower operating bills. It has better rustproofing, will last longer, will require less service, and among other things, it will operate quietly. Noisy operation is a common complaint about room coolers. Pay special attention to this when you buy. Turn various models on in the showroom, and compare their operating noise one against another.

A few other tips: Only buy a unit with the certification seal of the National Electrical Manufacturers Association (NEMA). Most brands carry this seal, but any unit without it could be a real clinker.

Be sure that the controls are easily accessible. See that the air louvers can be adjusted up and down and side to side for best cool-air distribution. Remove the filter. It should be easy to remove and clean and inexpensive to replace. Who will service the equipment? Find out about this beforehand, or you may find nobody around to fix it if trouble develops.

Should you get a model that requires 115 volts or 230 volts of electricity? A 230-volt model is better unless you have only 115 volts in your house. A 230-volt line may have to be installed from your electric board to a new outlet to provide sufficient power for the air-conditioner. This can be worth its cost, since a 230-volt unit is more efficient and cheaper to operate than a 115-volt cooler. A 115-volt model is recommended only if that's all the electricity you have and it will cost too much to install 230-volt power. If you must buy a 115-volt model, consider a high-efficiency, low-ampere type. It draws the least current, offers good operating efficiency, and is least 'likely to blow out your house fuses.

Room Air-conditioner Operating Costs

The operating cost of a typical room air-conditioner of about ten thousand B.t.u.'s per hour of capacity ordinarily runs about twenty dollars to twenty-five dollars a summer in the North and up to about forty dollars in the South. That's for electricity costing two cents per kilowatt hour. It breaks down to an average of six dollars to eight dollars a month. A larger unit with, say, fifteen thousand B.t.u.'s capacity will cost roughly 50 per cent more, smaller units proportionately less. If your electric rates are more or less than two cents per kilowatt hour, your operating cost will be proportionately more or less.

AIR-CONDITIONING REVIEW

If you now have air conditioning in your house, you probably can get better performance and lower its cost by reducing the heat load on the equipment and operating it efficiently.

The same measures for achieving economical air-conditioning can also help when you buy air conditioning for a house. Before buying, review the section in this chapter on the most common problems encountered with home air-conditioning, as well as the section on buying. This can greatly help you avoid the same problems and get the best system for your house.

CHAPTER 7   PROPERLY INSURING YOUR
HOUSE AND PERSONAL PROPERTY
AGAINST A MAJOR LOSS

■

*Determining the right amount of insurance for a house . . .
Reappraising your present insurance . . . Fire, theft, and personal-liability insurance . . . Choosing the best of the five different kinds of homeowners insurance . . . Do you have the
right theft, burglary, and liability coverage? . . . Special insurance for eight kinds of valuable personal property . . . Theft
protection away from home . . . How to save on home insurance
. . . Why the same insurance policies vary in cost among different companies . . . "Deductibles" that offer savings . . . What
to do before a fire or other loss and important steps to take
promptly after fire to cut your loss . . . How to settle a claim
. . . Buying insurance for the first time . . . When to replace
your present insurance . . . Buying mail-order insurance . . .
Choosing a good agent and a good company.*

About 500,000 houses in the United States catch fire every year.
Not all of them burn down, luckily. About 90 per cent are
covered by insurance. Unfortunately, however, as many as half
have the wrong kind of insurance or not enough of it. Lack of
proper insurance is the biggest cause of major financial loss to
homeowners after a fire, theft, or loss at home.

Not long ago, for example, the $24,000 house of a family in
a midwestern city burned down. The family collected $14,000
in insurance, since that was all the coverage they had. They
had bought the house fifteen years previously for $14,000 and
had put that much insurance on it. The house increased in value
over the years, largely because of inflation, but the owner ne-

glected to increase his insurance at the same rate. At the time of the fire the cost of rebuilding the house was $24,000; construction costs had risen that much since the house had been purchased.

Another illustration of what, alas, often happens is the story of what occurred a few years ago to a splendid 140-year-old summer home in upstate New York which belongs to the well-known American author Philip Wylie. Fire gutted the kitchen and damaged several nearby rooms. A total of $30,000 of damage was done, much of it from the smoke that poured through the house and from the water and chemicals sprayed into the house to put out the blaze. It was an expensive job to wash down the smoke-stained walls and clean up the water- and chemical-soaked house and furnishings, as well as repair the burned-out parts of the house.

Sad to say, Mr. Wylie had a mere $10,000 worth of insurance on the house. That, he said later, was "because the house would not have brought much more than that" at the time it was insured. He had to dig into his own pocket for the additional $20,000 for repairs. "We were appallingly underinsured," he said sadly.

Because of inflation many houses have increased two to four times in value since the end of World War II. A house built for $10,000 in 1950 would cost at least $20,000 to $30,000 to duplicate twenty years later in most parts of the country, and in some places it would cost as much as $40,000. This emphasizes one of the most important things to be aware of in order to avoid a major financial debacle even if you have insurance: Don't be underinsured. That goes for the insurance on household contents as well as on your house structure.

WHY HOME INSURANCE?

Home insurance protects you against a loss due to a house fire, smoke, the water and chemicals used to fight the fire, and against damage from such perils as windstorm, hail, vandalism, explosion, riot, ice, snow, broken glass, a fallen tree, bursting pipes, and theft and burglary. There is also personal-liability insurance to protect you if a person is accidentally hurt or seriously injured in your house, on your property, or by a member of your family.

Not everybody has all of these and other available coverages, and in fact not everyone may necessarily need them all. There are certain kinds of risks with a house—such as fire, for example —which virtually demand insurance protection. Many home-owners experience a loss due to fire or other mishap about once every five years.

HOW TO GET THE BEST HOME INSURANCE

Here is a summary of the best ways to get all the protection you need at the lowest cost, including how your present insurance can be changed or modified now, in midterm, at savings to you.

- Shop for the best price. Some companies charge 10 to 20 per cent less than other companies for the same insurance.
- Consolidate your fire, theft, and liability insurance into one homeowners policy. You may already have a homeowners policy, but do you have the best one of the different kinds available?
- Take advantage of all "deductible" options.
- Act promptly after a loss to prevent further loss.
- Follow through properly on a claim.
- Deal with a good insurance agent. (This is perhaps most important of all.)

A few basic facts about insurance should be understood. For example, your present insurance policy may have a year or two to run before renewal time, but you need not wait till then to make an important change. Changes can be made in almost any home policy in midterm without a penalty charge. The right change could even get you a refund now. Another important thing is knowing how to determine the amount of insurance you need.

HOW MUCH INSURANCE FOR YOUR HOUSE?

The key figure to determine is the present-day replacement cost of your house, the money you would need to rebuild the house if it burned to the ground. You exclude the cost of replacing the foundation and the underground water, sewer, and other utility lines from the street to the house. These generally do not have to be replaced after a fire. They account for about 10 per cent of the total construction cost of a house.

A good insurance agent can tell you how to figure the present replacement cost of your house, less foundation and less the cost of new underground utilities. If he can't, you may have to consult a good appraiser, builder, or local contractor, or you can ask your agent to provide you with a "building-cost calculator," used to estimate home-building costs for insurance purposes.

Do not use the market value of your house to determine your insurance. That's the price you may have recently paid to buy the house or the price you would get if you sold the house today.

Market value includes the value of your house lot (your land) in addition to the worth of the house. You might buy a house today for $32,000, say, but the land under it could account for $4,000, $6,000, or perhaps $8,000 of that, depending on its size and location. If it were worth $6,000, your house would be worth $26,000. Even this figure, $26,000, can be misleading as an indication of the amount of money that would be required to rebuild the house. You almost definitely do not want $32,000 of insurance, because it includes the value of your lot, which is irrelevant for insurance purposes. The proper figure, again, is the total replacement cost of the house itself.

80 Per Cent Insurance

You may not even need full replacement insurance, because the likelihood of a total loss to fire or other calamity may be small.

A total loss is most likely with a frame house located, for example, in a rural area with poor local fire protection and poor access to water. It's least likely with a brick or stone house with both a good fire department and a fire hydrant close by. You should balance the probabilities of a total loss against the cost of full insurance on your house. You can save money with insurance equal to 80 per cent of the house replacement cost: that means $24,000 of insurance at least for a $30,000 house (.80 times $30,000).

Don't go below 80 per cent. You need at least 80 per cent insurance to be paid in full for partial damage to your house. The house of one man sustained $4,000 worth of damage due to a storm that toppled an oak tree down on his house. He had a $25,000 insurance policy on the house, but the insurance company paid him only $3,472 for the damage. When the loss occurred, the replacement cost of the house was $36,000. His insurance amounted to less than 80 per cent of the replacement cost of the house, so he did not get full payment for the damage. This formula determined his payment:

$$\frac{\$25,000 \text{ insurance}}{\$28,800 \ (80\% \text{ of } \$36,000)} \times \$4,000 \ (\text{loss}) = \$3,472.$$

Nearly all house-insurance policies today stipulate that you will recover full replacement value up to the policy amount for loss *only* if your insurance is equal to at least 80 per cent of the cost of rebuilding the house. If you have less than 80 per cent, your settlement is based on the repair cost less depreciation.

Depreciation has to do with the assumed use you have received from your house or that part that suffers damage. Suppose a ten-year-old roof is damaged by a storm. Assume that the roof has a normal life of twenty years and a new roof will cost three thousand dollars. You'll collect only fifteen hundred dollars from the insurance company; i.e., three thousand dollars minus 50 per cent, or fifteen hundred dollars, for ten years' use. That's 50 per cent depreciation.

It's usually best to have a little more than 80 per cent insurance. Make it about 85 per cent to allow for creeping inflation during the three years your policy will be in force before renewal. Increase it a little each year to keep up with inflation, or ask your insurance man for an "inflation guard" clause, available in about forty states.

How much insurance do you have now? Does it meet the 80 per cent rule? Insurance people report that literally hundreds of thousands of homeowners—perhaps several million—carry insurance equal to less than 80 per cent of the replacement value of their houses. They could sustain a grievous loss.

WHAT KIND OF INSURANCE?

Buying house insurance is like buying building blocks. The cheapest, most minimal policy—the first block—is a standard fire policy that protects you against loss from fire and lightning. Next is a policy with extended coverage, which also covers you for damage from wind, hail, smoke, and about ten more perils in all. Then comes an additional block of insurance added to the same policy for a little more money, of course. It extends your coverage so you're also protected from loss from eight more perils, including damage from a broken water or steam pipe, frozen pipes, and falling trees. This is called the broad form. Similarly, there are other insurance polices for theft and personal-liability insurance. To them you can add building blocks to give you additional coverage for theft and liability.

Insurance for houses is also packaged in single homeowners policies, economically tailored for people who want the three main kinds of home insurance—fire and extended coverage, theft, and personal liability—all in one policy. It's a three-in-one policy that usually costs less than the same insurance bought with separate policies.

The homeowners policy, introduced in 1952 in the United States, has caught on widely. It now accounts for about 60 to 70 per cent of all insurance on houses. A homeowners "tenants" policy is also available for those who rent. There are five kinds of homeowners policies, each one going up a step with a block of additional insurance. Here is what they are:

1. *The Homeowners 1, or HO-1.* It's also called the standard, or Homeowners A. It gives minimal insurance on your house plus insurance for theft and personal-liability protection. (This last protects you not only if someone is seriously hurt in your house or on your property but also, for example, if one of your family accidentally injures someone on a golf course or anywhere else away from home (except in your car). An HO-1 is recommended only if you're on a very limited budget and every single dollar counts.

2. *The Homeowners 2, or HO-2.* Also called the Homeowners B, this is the next step up. It combines the broad-form fire policy with theft and personal-liability coverage. It costs about 10 per cent more than the H-1 for considerably more coverage, and it is usually worth it. Most people should have at least this much insurance.

3. *Homeowners 3, or HO-3.* Also called the B-plus, sometimes it's called the 3-plus-4 policy; to confuse things even more, insurance people may call it the special form. It's the policy that many insurance experts choose for their own houses. It costs about 15 per cent more than the HO-2. For that you get "all-risk" insurance on your house structure. Think of your insurance as being divided into two parts. One part protects the house structure, a separate garage, and, within certain limits, the trees, shrubs, and other buildings on your land. The second part of the insurance covers your personal possessions, including clothing, furniture, and everything you would take with you if you moved. For insurance purposes these two categories—house and property versus household possessions—are separated from each other.

The all-risk feature of the HO-3 applies only to the first category, damage to your house structure. It's a big step forward in this coverage, compared with the HO-2 policy. It insures you against a great variety of things that could happen which are not specifically named in the policy. Among them could be a cracked ceiling as a result of nearby blasting or the unusual damage caused by a teen-age scientist in Illinois who left a pan of paraffin heating over his Bunsen burner. The paraffin boiled and steamed through the house, causing more than a thousand dollars' damage to the walls and ceilings where it landed. The cleanup cost was paid by his family's HO-3 all-risk policy. They would not have collected with an HO-1 or HO-2 policy (because these insure you only for damage caused by one of the perils specifically stipulated in the policy and listed later in this chapter).

The HO-3 offers another benefit. If your house is damaged and a dispute arises over your claim, the burden of proof falls on the company. It must prove that the damage was caused by one of the specific perils not covered by the policy. With an ordinary fire policy or HO-1 or HO-2 policy a similar dispute requires that you (the policyholder) prove that the damage is clearly and specifically covered in the policy. Insurance people often choose the HO-3 for their homes, since it can avoid a hassle over a claim because of its all-risk provisions. That is probably the principal reason that the same policy is recommended for others. Like other homeowners policies, the HO-3 also includes theft and personal-liability insurance.

4. *The Homeowners 4, or HO-4.* The HO-4, also called the tenants policy, is the insurance package for those who rent a house or apartment and want theft and personal-liability insurance in addition to fire insurance for personal property. Your household contents are protected not only against damage or loss caused by fire but also against the variety of other perils covered in the HO-2 policy, but you pay less because there is no insurance on the house structure.

5. *The Homeowners 5, or HO-5.* Known also as the C policy, this is the deluxe homeowners policy, the Cadillac of the species. It's also called the comprehensive form. It's generally 50 to 100 per cent higher in price than an HO-3 policy. It can be expensive, in other words, but it gives you all-risk insurance on all personal property in addition to all-risk coverage on your

house structure. You are protected against any damage or loss to your personal property as well as to your house unless it is caused by one of those nine specific exclusions that are also excluded in the HO-3 (damage due to a flood, landslide, tidal wave, and so on).

Because of its cost, an HO-5 policy is generally not recommended unless you have a lot of expensive furnishings and furniture or you travel a lot, often taking valuable personal property with you. In the first case, the deluxe HO-5 policy gives you comprehensive insurance for nearly any kind of unpredictable damage or loss to your furnishings and household possessions. In the second case, the policy by and large gives you considerably more insurance than any other homeowners policy on your personal property (expensive luggage, clothing, and other possessions but *not* on your jewelry and furs) that you take with you when away from home.

You should not count on an HO-5 or any other homeowners policy to insure valuable paintings, furs, jewelry, or other personal property of high value. Valuable belongings should be insured in a special way, which will be described in a moment.

HOW MUCH INSURANCE FOR PERSONAL PROPERTY?

Obviously, the amount of personal-property insurance you hold should be enough to cover you in case of a major loss. Like your house structure, personal property is covered in a homeowners policy against loss or damage by fire and the other perils cited in the policy. It's covered up to a total of 50 per cent of the house coverage. A thirty-thousand-dollar homeowners policy on your house covers your personal property up to fifteen thousand dollars, a forty-thousand-dollar policy gives you twenty thousand dollars of coverage on personal property, and so on. That means, by the way, that you could collect more than forty thousand dollars with a forty-thousand-dollar policy. If a fire destroyed your house and everything in it, you could collect up to sixty

Typical Three-Year Costs for $25,000 Homeowners Policies

Here are the costs of homeowners policies for a frame house. Each policy includes the $50-deductible clauses available in the area except for the HO-5 policy, which includes $100 deductibles.

Suburbs of	HO-1, or A Policy	HO-2, or B Policy	HO-3, or B-Plus Policy	HO-5, or C Policy
Atlanta, Ga.	$264	$345	$381	$690
Boston, Mass.	$325	$409	$446	$881
Chicago, Ill.	$192	$252	$285	$576
Denver, Col.	$219	$260	$288	$544
New York, N.Y.	$307	$428	$465	$900
San Francisco, Cal.	$312	$372	$399	$861

thousand dollars: forty thousand dollars for the house and up to twenty thousand dollars more for the personal-property loss.

Underinsurance on personal property is as widespread as under-insurance on houses, if not more so. That 50 per cent personal-property coverage is often not enough, considering the broad array of family possessions in many houses today. A modern kitchen and laundry may contain several thousand dollars of appliances and other apparatus. Add up the value of all other such items, plus clothing and furnishings, and the total value of your personal property could surprise you. If it's more than your present coverage (50 per cent of your total policy coverage with a homeowners policy), consider increasing this part of your insurance. The cost to increase personal-property coverage in a homeowners policy runs about two to four dollars for each one thousand dollars of extra insurance. That's to increase only your personal-property coverage; the insurance on your house and other coverages in the policy remain the same.

Unlike the insurance on a house, which can pay you the full amount to rebuild a damaged house, insurance paid for a per-sonal-property loss is based on depreciated value. Payment for loss of a fur coat or damaged sofa or rug, for example, would be based on the present value of the item minus the value you have already received from it. One woman we know lost a five-year-old sofa because of a cigarette fire. The sofa had an estimated normal life of fifteen years and was worth $420 new. She was paid $280 by the insurance company, which was the depreciated value of the sofa. That's two thirds of its replacement cost. The woman had received one third of its value in five years of use.

Take depreciation into account when you make an inventory of your household possessions. The total price you paid for everything you now own might add up to $22,000, for example. Because of depreciation, varying from item to item, the present-day value of your personal property might amount to $16,000. That $16,000 is the most you would be paid by the insurance company, and it is therefore the amount of insurance you should have, not $22,000.

HOMEOWNERS POLICY REVIEW

Here is a brief summary of the protection given with each of the five homeowners policies.

Homeowners 1 (HO-1): Your house structure, outside property, and personal property (household contents) are protected against damage or loss from:
1. Fire and lightning
2. Property moved from your premises in case of fire
3. Wind, storm, and hail
4. Explosion
5. Riot or civil commotion
6. Aircraft
7. Runaway cars, trucks, or other vehicles (not owned or driven by a member of your household)
8. Smoke or smudge from a cooking or heating unit (but not from a fireplace)
9. Vandalism and malicious mischief
10. Broken glass (up to $50)
11. Theft

Damage to your house or personal property by any cause other than those listed above is not covered.

Loss to personal property (not part of house structure) is covered up to 50 per cent of the house coverage. If your house burns to the ground, you are paid the full policy amount on the dwelling—say, $25,000 for the house—and you may get as much as $12,500 more for personal-property loss.

Damage to other buildings, such as a detached garage or tool shed, is covered up to 10 per cent of the house insurance.

Damage to plants, trees, shrubs, lawn, and such is included up to 5 per cent of house coverage but for no more than $250 per item (and not for wind, frost, snow, or insect damage).

Personal-liability coverage up to $25,000 is also provided by this and all other homeowners policies.

Homeowners 2 (HO-2): You are protected against all eleven of the hazards listed above plus damage or loss from:

12. Falling objects, such as icicles, trees, and branches

13. Weight of ice, snow, or sleet, causing structural collapse

14. Sudden accidental damage to electrical appliances or electrical equipment, fixtures, and wiring (TV picture tube excluded)

15. Explosion, cracking, or burning of a steam or hot-water heating system or water-heater

16. Water or steam accidentally escaping from plumbing, heating, or air conditioning

17. Frozen pipes (if you have exercised "due care" to prevent such an occurrence)

18. Structural collapse *except* if caused by landslide, flood, tidal wave, termites, or earthquake

Earthquake coverage can be had as an extra here and in other policies. Government-sponsored flood insurance is also available now in some parts of the country and is expected to become more widely available in the future. If flooding is a peril to your house, ask your insurance agent about this coverage. Coverage for the other exclusions under item 18 is virtually impossible to get except at prohibitive cost.

Homeowners 3 (HO-3): This covers all eighteen items listed above plus most other accidental losses *except* damage caused by the following perils:

a. Flood, surface water, waves, and tidal water
b. Backup of sewer pipes or drainpipes and water seepage
c. War and nuclear radiation
d. Mechanical breakdowns
e. Normal wear and deterioration
f. Inherent structural defects
g. Smog and smoke damage from smudge pots and factories
h. Landslide
i. Earthquake (unless added by special endorsement)

Personal property gets the same coverage in the HO-3 as in the HO-2; i.e., you're protected against damage from perils 1 through 18 only.

Homeowners 4 (HO-4): The tenants policy offers the same personal-property insurance as in Homeowners 2 but without coverage on the dwelling.

Homeowners 5 (HO-5): This provides the same house coverage as in HO-3 above plus extensive personal-property insurance up to 50 per cent of the house policy for all accidental losses, though there are a few exclusions.

Homeowners insurance is sold in every state except Mississippi. In Mississippi comparable insurance can be had with what is called a comprehensive-dwelling policy. Like the homeowners policy, it includes fire, theft, and personal-liability coverage.

OTHER INSURANCE POLICIES

In addition to homeowners policies, there are other kinds of insurance sold for houses. If you have more than one of the following policies, you might do better if you switched to a comprehensive homeowners policy.

Standard fire policy: This protects your house only against fire and lightning damage. A fire policy with extended coverage is usually better. That protects you from damage from such things as wind and hail, riot, and the other additional perils covered in a HO-1 policy and noted earlier. It's even better to extend your coverage to the 18 perils covered in an HO-2 policy.

Dwelling and contents form: This gives you roughly the same insurance on both your house and personal property as you get in an HO-1 policy except for no coverage for theft and personal liability.

Dwelling building(s) and contents broad form: This is equivalent to the same insurance on your house and personal property as given in an HO-2 policy but with no theft and personal-liability coverage.

Dwelling building(s) special form: This is all-risk insurance on your house only, as in the HO-3, but no insurance on your personal possessions and property.

HOW MUCH PERSONAL-LIABILITY INSURANCE SHOULD YOU HAVE?

Personal-liability insurance is important insurance. It protects you from a disaster that might be the biggest financial setback you could ever suffer from. It's like hitting the jackpot in reverse.

The probability of such a disaster is small, but if it happens, your jackpot loss could be huge. It could happen if, for example, a child was hurt seriously in your backyard, if a mailman had a bad fall down your front steps, or if a member of your family, while away from home, hooked another person in the eye with a fishing fly. If a serious injury resulted, you could be liable to the tune of $50,000 to $100,000, or possibly more, considering the high awards that juries make nowadays.

It happened to a midwestern family when a mailman tripped on a child's roller skate left out front. He broke his back and was paralyzed for life. A jury awarded him a $78,000 judgment. The family's insurance company paid $25,000, the standard coverage in homeowners policies, and the homeowner had to pay the rest.

It took all his life savings plus a hefty bite out of his pay check every week for more than twenty years until the judgment was paid off.

True, you are held accountable only if you are proven negligent in causing such an accident. But this is a sticky point. Any doubt about it is often settled in favor of the injured person. That's why more than the minimum $25,000 of liability insurance is often recommended for many families. Your coverage can be increased to $100,000 or as much as $500,000 for a comparatively small extra premium. If you are a family in modest financial circumstances with slim possibility of a liability action against you, consider increasing it to at least $100,000; more if the odds are higher against you.

Your liability increases if you entertain frequently, have active children, or, among other things, have a large property with potential hazards such as a swimming pool or waterfront location. It also increases if you golf or ski or engage in any activity which means possible contact with other people.

Moreover, the more affluent you are, the greater your potential liability. That's because you automatically become a special target for a big law suit. An opposing lawyer often figures he can collect more from a family that is well-off or seems to be (such as a doctor or business executive) than from a family in modest circumstances (such as a teacher or white-collar worker).

The liability coverage in an existing homeowners policy can be increased by calling your insurance agent and having him boost this coverage. The extra premium cost depends on the increased coverage and where you live. Here are the approximate additional annual premiums for increased liability insurance if you already have a homeowners policy with the standard $25,000 liability coverage:

Personal Liability	New York State	Ohio	California
$100,000	$10–$12	$3–$4	$4–$6
$200,000	$13–$15	$5–$6	$6–$8
$300,000	$16–$20	$7–$9	$8–$11

The cost is highest in New York State because the size and frequency of liability awards are highest there. Your insurance man can quickly tell you what the cost would be in your state. If you have neither a homeowners policy nor a separate personal-liability policy, the cost is more.

Medical Payments

The personal-liability part of most homeowners policies also covers you for up to $250 to $500 worth of medical payments. That's to pay the doctor bill if someone is hurt while visiting your house or if a member of your family had something to do with an injury to another person or, among other things, if your dog bites someone. The fault may or may not be yours. In either case, this built-in protection means that the insurance company will pay the medical bills for the other person. It's not paid, however, if a member of your family is hurt; it's paid only for an injury to a nonmember of your household. You sometimes can save a dollar or two a year by dropping the coverage to $250, or the limit can be raised to $1,000 coverage for about a dollar or two a year extra premium.

THEFT INSURANCE

Losses from theft (including burglaries) account for the third largest cause of losses to homeowners after fire and wind-storm damage. Theft ranks first, however, in terms of number of controversies over insurance and claims.

A homeowners policy gives you roughly the same insurance against theft that you would get in a separate home-theft policy. If your house is burglarized of personal property, your insurance covers the loss up to 50 per cent of your homeowner house coverage, just as it does for a personal-property loss due to another cause. A thirty-thousand-dollar policy therefore covers you for a loss of personal possessions worth up to fifteen thousand dollars.

There are a few catches, however. Theft of jewelry, watches, and furs is covered only up to five hundred dollars, in all, no matter what the total value of the loss. Ceilings are also put on the coverage for cash stolen from you (one hundred dollars top insurance payment) and on such valuables as stocks and bonds, I.O.U. notes, a valuable stamp collection, and so on (usually five hundred dollars top coverage).

Special Insurance for Valuables

Moral: If you own such valuables, don't count on the standard homeowners policy to protect you against a major theft. The standard homeowners policy, designed for the majority of home-owners with a limited number of valuable possessions, clearly gives limited insurance for valuables. If you have valuable posses-sions, you might do well to consider special insurance for them. You can get this, at an extra price, naturally, with a Personal Articles Floater (PAF), which is a supplement to a homeowners policy. A PAF can be used to insure eight different items:

1. Diamonds and jewelry
2. Furs
3. Silverware
4. Cameras and photographic equipment
5. Fine arts, including antiques, heirlooms, statuary, sculptures, paintings
6. Sporting equipment
7. Musical instruments
8. Stamp collections
9. Coin collections

The annual cost of adding a PAF rider to a homeowners policy varies according to the item and where you live. Insuring a fur coat may run from 30¢ per $100 of insurance in a midwestern city up to four times as much in Chicago or New York (where thieves make off with many more furs). Diamonds and jewelry can range from under $1 per $100 of value up to $2.50 per $100, depending on where you live. If you own an original Picasso, you will pay about 20¢ to 30¢ per $100 of value per year. A lower rate is charged for objects of art than for other more portable valuables because they are less likely to be lost or stolen away from home and there is hence less risk for the insurance company.

Pitfalls to Avoid

A PAF should cover the full worth of the item insured. Don't assume that your regular homeowners policy insures the item up to $500 and therefore a valuable necklace worth $1,500, for example, only needs an additional $1,000 of PAF insurance. If the necklace is lost or stolen, you'll be paid only $1,000, not the full $1,500.

That's because a PAF policy for a valuable automatically removes the same article from any coverage by your regular homeowners policy. In short, don't count on your homeowners policy to provide partial insurance on a valuable in addition to separate PAF coverage on the item.

A second pitfall to avoid is failure to review periodically the insurance on valuables. This can cost you money coming and going, since possessions can vary in value from year to year. A fur coat, for example, depreciates in value each year. Reduce the insurance on it as it does, and save on the premium.

On the other hand, a diamond necklace, an antique, and especially a good painting can grow in value over the years, sometimes steeply. This calls for an annual reappraisal of their insured value. You will have to pay a larger premium, but without it you risk a larger loss.

One woman we know lost a diamond ring that had been insured for $2,400 when she got it ten years earlier. The insurance company paid her that amount, the full value of the policy. At the time her husband gave her the ring its diamonds were appraised at $6 a point. Ten years later when the ring was lost the diamonds had increased in value to $10 a point. Her ring was worth $4,000 at the time of loss, but because she had neglected to increase her insurance, she was paid only $2,400.

Is the insurance on your jewelry and other valuables right for what it should be today? This goes for silverware, antiques, cameras, and everything else noted above.

Off-Premises Theft

Personal property that is stolen from you when you are away from home is insured in most, though not all, homeowners policies for up to $1,000 or 10 per cent of your at-home coverage, whichever is larger. This includes clothing or golf clubs stolen from your car while on vacation, furniture stolen from a summer house, or any other possessions you have with you away from home.

If, for example, you have a $30,000 homeowners policy, all your personal property is ordinarily covered up to $15,000 (50 per cent). But theft away from home is covered up to $1,500 (10 per cent of $15,000). An exception is the deluxe HO-5 policy which insures you for up to 100 per cent of your at-home coverage. Thus a $30,000 HO-5 policy gives you up to $15,000 coverage (50 per cent of $30,000) for theft of personal property away from home.

Not all homeowners policies give away-from-home theft coverage. This coverage is omitted from some policies for people who live in a high-risk, high-theft area, such as New York City and nearby. (Coverage can, however, be added in such places for an additional premium.) Unfortunately, all you can do then is not leave clothing and valuables in your car and not carry a lot of cash on you (i.e., cut down your exposure to a theft). You could also get a PAF rider that would cover your valuable items both at home and away.

Summed up, a homeowners policy can give you reasonably good theft insurance for the usual personal property. It gives quite limited coverage, however, on valuables. Furnishings and other possessions kept at a summer house are a special case that varies from family to family, particularly possessions left there the year around. Check the coverage you may need with your insurance man.

HOW TO SAVE MONEY ON HOME INSURANCE

Reappraise your present policies. If you now have a regular fire policy and one or more other policies for theft and personal liability, a comparable homeowners policy would probably give you comparable insurance protection for less money. A home-owners policy sometimes offers even more coverage at lower cost.

Remember that one can switch to a different policy at any time. If you switch, try to buy your new policy from the same company with whom you're canceling an old policy. You'll get a greater credit for the unexpired premium on your old policy. If you switch to a policy with another company, you do not get a full refund on the unexpired part of the canceled policy. You could lose money here on a "short-rated" refund. Nonetheless, the savings on a new homeowners policy plus the added protection it can give you will usually offset that loss.

Not everyone needs a homeowners policy. Some people may not need theft or liability insurance. A fire policy, preferably with extended coverage, might be all you need. That could be the case, for example, if you have no personal possessions of great value and you live in a small town or rural area where theft and burglary are rare. Or you may live in an apartment with no children and own no property for which you are liable. You live a sedentary life with little possibility of an action of yours causing injury to another person. Your need for liability insurance may be very small, if not nil.

A simple fire policy and possibly one for theft or liability may then be all you need. You then save money, compared with the cost of a full-fledged homeowners policy. If you now have a home-owners policy, you could turn it in for the more limited separate insurance. Stay with the same insurance company, if possible, at least until the new insurance must be renewed. Then switch to another company, if desired.

Choose the best homeowners policy for your needs. Assume, for example, that you now have a deluxe homeowners HO-5. Do you really need it? If you have it chiefly to protect valuables like jewelry and furs, you will often save money by switching to an HO-2 or HO-3 and taking out individual floaters for your valuables. On the other hand, you may have an HO-1 or HO-2 policy but would get better protection by stepping up to the next higher homeowners policy. You'd pay a higher premium, but you'd be protecting yourself against a major loss not covered in your present policy.

Take all the deductible options you can. They generally offer considerable savings. They mean, of course, that you absorb from $50 to as much as $500 of a loss, and the company pays you the balance, as with car insurance. They can reduce your annual insurance premium by 25 to 30 per cent.

All home-insurance policies in some states must contain certain deductible clauses; you have no choice. In others, the deductible clauses are optional; it's up to the buyer to take them or not. You should ask about them for three good reasons. The annual savings on your premiums are more than likely to offset an occasional $50 or so loss on a possible claim. In one state, for example, you pay $391 for a three-year homeowners policy with no deductibles but only $274 for the same policy with $50 deductible. That's $117 saved in three years, or more than you are likely to lose due to loss or damage to your house.

Secondly, and unlike car insurance, this kind of deductible is usually—though not always—a "disappearing deductible." The greater your claim, the smaller the amount deducted by the insurance company. On a $200 loss the insurance company deducts only $33.50, instead of the full $50 deductible; on a $300 loss it deducts only $22.50; and generally there's no deductible on a claim for $500 or more. That's the case with the $50 deductible clause in nearly all states except New York and New Hampshire (where it's a flat deductible taken out in full by the company).

There are also $100, $250, and $500 optional deductibles which are flat, not disappearing, deductibles. The whole amount is deducted from a claim check. These higher deductibles can also cut your insurance cost by another 25 per cent a year. By and large, you should save over the long term.

Third, the deductible often does not apply to a loss caused by theft or a liability loss, and it may or may not apply to fire, lightning, and other damage, depending on your state insurance rules. You would get full payment for such losses. If your present insurance does not include deductibles, adding them now might mean a refund for you.

Know what to do promptly after a loss. Phone your agent or insurance company at once. Call long distance collect, if necessary. Do this if anyone is hurt on your property and after a burglary, theft, or fire, and notify the police too.

Take measures to hold down the damage, especially after a fire. Cover a hole in the roof, close the windows against rain, wipe water off furniture, and start cleaning up promptly. Separate damaged from undamaged property, but don't throw away the debris.

If the furnace is knocked out during cold weather, have it repaired fast, or install portable heaters. Water hosed on a house to put out a fire can accumulate inside walls and freeze, compounding your troubles.

These and other things to do are spelled out in the first section of a homeowners policy and on lines 90 to 122 of the standard house-fire policy. If more damage occurs that you might have prevented, your insurance often will not cover the additional damage.

Know all the losses you're covered for. A homeowners policy insures you against certain losses that many people are unaware of. An example is coverage for a theft away from home (which we've mentioned), like an overcoat stolen from a coat rack in a restaurant. You're also paid outside living expenses in a motel or anywhere else if you're forced out of your house because of a fire or other damage. When a tornado struck a Kansas town not long ago, nearly two thousand people, temporarily homeless, collected $1.5 million dollars in insurance for hotel bills, food, and other such expenses. You're also paid for damage accidentally inflicted on a neighbor's property or, say, equipment you borrow from him and accidentally break and for a variety of other losses.

Don't, however, consider your insurance policy a home-maintenance contract. It may cover many small losses to your house, and some people file frequent "nickel-and-dime" claims. This is not recommended. They are a nuisance, and the claims are expensive to process. Such people build themselves a bad record with their insurance companies, which could boomerang on them later. The real purpose of insurance is to protect you against a major loss. You're entitled, of course, to collect for any bona fide loss, small or large, but you should concentrate on protection against major losses. Read the policy to know about every coverage you have. (To be sure, the language is often difficult to understand, if not virtually incomprehensible here and there. This is an area in which the insurance companies could improve things considerably.)

Be prepared for a loss. Take photographs of your house, inside and out. Keep them in your office or in a safe-deposit box (not in the house, of course). The pictures could be valuable later in helping you prove what was lost in a fire and also in helping you get an accurate inventory of your loss.

Keep an up-to-date inventory, too, of personal possessions and household contents with their estimated value. Take photographs of these, too. These should also be kept elsewhere. Doing an inventory can be a chore, to be sure; it's one of those things we know we should do but often put off. You'll have to provide one later, however, after a loss, and then it will be considerably harder.

Purchase bills and receipts for personal property should be kept. To be paid full value for loss of personal property—especially furs, jewelry, heirlooms, and antiques—you will have to prove its value. That usually requires either a purchase bill or an appraisal by an expert.

Know how to settle a claim properly. This is the moment of truth, a time of negotiation during which you could gain or lose substantially. A company adjuster will ordinarily visit you to appraise your loss and make a settlement offer. Before he does, and at least before you accept the offer, arm yourself with facts and evidence. If house repairs are required, you may have to get estimates for the work. As we just noted, the loss of personal property and household contents will require proof of the value of the loss.

Many disputes center on the value of personal property, and here's where those records, an inventory, and purchase invoices can be of great help. Don't put yourself trustfully and completely in the hands of the adjuster, however friendly he may be. You're involved in a business matter. Many adjusters try to be scrupulously fair. They follow a regular procedure in estimating losses. Some may make you an initial low bid on the principle that negotiations will follow; they want to allow for raising their bid.

Don't deal with the adjuster with a chip-on-your-shoulder attitude. Don't be cocky or smart alecky; this is the worst thing you can do, especially if arguments and open warfare follow. The adjuster, being human (most are), is likely to stiffen with resistance and fight back just as hard. Keep your cool.

Consult an expert or two—your family lawyer and your insurance man—and you should get a good idea of what you should be paid for your loss. If an impasse develops, serious negotiations may be required. A good professional public insurance adjuster might help here by negotiating the best possible settlement. If you anticipate trouble settling, particularly for a large loss, call in a PIA early.

Books have been written about settling insurance claims, and you might study a few. One is *Sue or Settle?*, by Robert W. Constantin, $3.95, published by Crown Publishers, Inc., which should be available at a bookstore or library.

BUYING INSURANCE AT THE BEST PRICE

Here's what to know when you buy new home insurance and also when your present insurance expires and must be renewed. That's the best time to switch to another company, if desired.

Shop around and you'll find that the price of the same insurance policy can vary as much as 10 to 20 per cent from company to company. (Most companies use standard state-approved policy forms, nearly all of which are from the same printing press.) That could mean savings of up to twenty dollars to thirty dollars a year for a homeowners HO-2 policy for the average house.

The cost generally varies according to the kind of company. The lowest cost is generally charged by companies that sell direct through their own company-employed agents. These include companies like Kemper, Nationwide Mutual, and State Farm Mutual.

Some mutual companies and a few nonmutuals charge the standard state-wide "bureau" rates but will pay you a dividend at the end of the year. A mutual company is owned, in effect, by its policyholders rather than by stockholders. When it earns a "profit," the excess money is returned to the policyholders in the form of a dividend. The dividend is not guaranteed, but when given it is equal to a discount on your premium. It can range from 1 or 2 per cent of your annual premium up to 20 per cent. Its size depends on the total claim money paid out by the company during the year, a dividend being declared when the claims don't exhaust the funds. In recent years some companies have lost money and therefore omitted dividends. Companies that give dividends off and on include Atlantic Mutual, Liberty Mutual, and Lumbermans Insurance Co.

There are also companies that sell through local insurance brokers who are not employed directly by the company. These include the two Aetna companies, Hartford, Continental Insurance, and Royal Globe, among others. These and many other national and regional companies generally sell their insurance at the same "bureau," or standard list-price, rates filed with each state. (The so-called bureau rate is the standard rate charged by a number of insurance companies whose rates are filed by their insurance "bureau.") You may pay a little more for their insurance, but they offer the advantage of dealing with a local insurance broker who may know your community well and be more familiar with local matters than a company-employed agent with a direct-selling insurance company.

Which company should you buy from? Balance the price charged against the service offered. Most important, however, deal only with a really reliable company that will stand behind its responsibility to you.

More than eight hundred different companies sell homeowners insurance, and as a rule it's better to buy from one of the larger companies. They are more likely to have experience in the various categories covered by a homeowners policy (theft, liability, and fire) than a small company that may be a specialist in only one or two of these categories.

To get prompt and efficient service on a claim, you should generally deal with a company that is active in your area; i.e., one that sells a lot of homeowners insurance locally. It can also help if it's a company whose headquarters are located in your part of the country or at least one that has a large regional office near you. In general, this means it may not help you to buy from a company located in California if you live in Boston, or vice versa, especially if the nearest regional office is in Dallas.

That's not an iron-clad rule. A number of national companies provide excellent service throughout the country, irrespective of the location of their headquarters. On the other hand, a company that is particularly experienced in your area can offer distinct advantages compared with a company that is not. For example, its adjusters, dealing every day with local fires and other losses, have a greater store of knowledge and experience with local building costs and various losses that may be peculiar to your part of the country and are not so frequent elsewhere.

Sometimes a small regional company offers specialized knowledge and ability that would be good for you. This is particularly true in New England and, among other places, in upper New York State, where a number of regional companies do a bang-up job. That kind of company where you live could well be the best bet for you, even though it does not advertise on national television.

Buy by Mail?

As a general rule, do *not* buy insurance by mail. Buy only from a company licensed to sell insurance in your state. Many mail-order companies can sell you insurance by mail with no license from your state, and many do. That could open a Pandora's box of troubles. You would, for example, have little or no recourse in case of a claim dispute, and some mail-order insurance companies are notorious for their questionable dealings. A company licensed to do business in your state not only must conform with your state laws, but the state insurance department also could go to bat for you in case of a dispute. The state officials are helpless, however, if the company is not licensed by them. (This, by the way, goes for automobile and life insurance, too.)

The tempting advantage of mail-order insurance is that it seems to offer low prices, but this is not necessarily so. You can almost always buy homeowners insurance as cheaply from a company that sells through agents or brokers. That goes for GEICO (Government Employees Insurance Company), one of the largest and best known mail-order insurance companies, and one of the reputable ones. A company like GEICO does offer low rates through the mail, but they are little or no lower than those offered by some low-cost direct-selling companies. Buying from such a company could be good if, among other things, you live in a small town or rural area where good insurance men are hard to find. But before buying from GEICO or any other mail-order company, find out where its nearest adjusters are located. What is the procedure for settling a claim? What would happen, for example, if your house burned to the ground? Must you negotiate the claim by mail, too?

DEAL WITH A GOOD AGENT OR BROKER

A careless agent could cost you dearly. A good agent, on the other hand, can help you get the best insurance at the right price. He should, as we've noted, know how to figure the present-day replacement cost of your house or get it figured so that you're adequately insured. He should counsel you about such things as when your insurance should be raised because of inflation or lowered for another reason.

Has your agent suggested such things recently? Has he advised you about the savings with deductibles, suggested periodic checks on your coverage, advised switching from separate policies to a homeowners? If he has, he's doing a good job, even though you may have brushed off his attempts to help. If he has not and you have doubts about him, you might do well to get another agent.

Ask for the names of good agents from people whose opinions you value—perhaps your lawyer, banker, or another local businessman. Seek an agent (or local firm) with at least four or five years of experience; preferably choose one who is well established locally. Be sure to deal with a full-time insurance man, not one who is also a real-estate agent or dogcatcher on the side.

Also, concentrate all of your casualty insurance with one good man and preferably with one company. That means buying both your car and home insurance and other casualty insurance you need from him. If he's also a good life-insurance expert—not all are—consider buying that, or part of it, from him too. The more insurance you buy from an agent, the more service you can expect from him. He'll put out greater effort for you when it otherwise would not be worth his time.

In general, you'll get more personal attention if you deal with an independent local insurance broker rather than an insurance-company agent. That's important if you don't want to be bothered by details but simply want all your insurance needs handled promptly and efficiently by an expert. You may pay a few dollars more, compared with dealing with a salaried agent working for a large direct-seller insurance company, but that's the small extra price you pay for maximum personal service.

It's good to concentrate your house, car, and other insurance with one good company for much the same reason. And the longer you keep your insurance with a company, the better. You build up good will that can make a world of difference when you have a claim. You're more likely to get the benefit of the doubt if a dispute arises. The company figures that since you've done right by them, they can do right by you. This is not necessarily always true, but it is often enough to make it good advice. And a long record with a company should be discreetly pointed out, if necessary, to the adjuster, who has come to settle a claim.

If, on the other hand, you shop for the lowest price, you should know more about what you're buying. Is the lower price for the same policy, or is it a lower price for less coverage on your house? Don't expect too much personal service and attention when you buy low-cost insurance from a company-employed agent. Nonetheless, the insurance is good provided you get the right policy for your needs.

INSURANCE FOR A NEW HOUSE

Arrange for your own insurance. Sometimes, in fact, you can transfer the policy on your present house to the new house, which could save you money. That's if you buy a house in the same state. If you move to another state, you might also save by arranging for the new insurance with the same company with whom you had the insurance on your last house.

The conditional sales contract generally signed to buy a house usually stipulates that the buyer agrees to take over the existing insurance on the house. You take pot luck here. This statement ordinarily should be struck out before you sign. Leave yourself the right to choose your own insurance.

Sometimes the builder of the house or the bank giving you the mortgage will offer to arrange for your insurance. It may be a genuinely helpful gesture, or it may not be. To play safe, check the insurance against what you could get yourself. You'll often find that you or your own broker can arrange your own insurance often at a lower price . . . and you might get better insurance, too.

HOW TO PAY FOR INSURANCE

Most home policies run for three years and then are renewed. You can pay for it all at once, getting up the total three-year premium when you buy, or pay in three annual installments or space out the payments in smaller monthly or semiannual payments.

Annual payments are often the best compromise. Paying off the insurance with smaller installments usually costs more, since a service charge is added to each payment (largely to cover the company's cost for extra billing). Paying the total three-year premium all at once will cost a few dollars less compared with three annual payments, but this is a deceptive saving. Pay one year at a time, and the balance of that three-year cost kept in your own bank could earn you more interest than you would otherwise save by paying it all at once. Paying once a year is also advantageous if you buy from a company that issues annual dividends. You will receive the dividend, when and if given, each year rather than at the end of every three years.

CREDIT-CARD INSURANCE

This is an optional extra you can usually buy if you now have a homeowners HO-2 to HO-5 policy. It protects you against loss if a credit or charge card is stolen or lost and then illegally used to run up bills on your account. This coverage also gives you "Depositors Forgery" insurance, which means you are protected if someone forges your name to a check or other financial paper that might cost you money. Ordinarily your bank is responsible if one of your checks is forged and they cash it. Sometimes, however, there might be a question about it. Then this insurance could save you. You are also protected if you are stuck with a counterfeit bill. Turn in the bogus bill to your insurance company and you are paid in cash up to the limit of your policy.

All of this goes with a credit-card insurance rider added to your policy. It may or may not be good for you. The cost is about four dollars a year for one thousand dollars of such insurance up to about eight dollars a year for ten thousand dollars insurance. You choose the amount you want.

Credit-card insurance, however, may or may not be desirable because of the federal credit-card law that went into effect early in 1971. It puts a fifty-dollar ceiling on the money you're liable for if an "unauthorized" person runs up charges on one of your cards.

Nevertheless, the law spells out certain conditions that could conceivably leave you vulnerable to a greater loss if one of your cards is lost or stolen. These conditions should be noted in the literature received from the company issuing each of your credit cards (or ask them for it). Credit-card insurance may still be desirable for the bank-forgery and counterfeit-bill protection it gives you, in addition to its credit-card protection. It's up to you to decide.

You are also now not liable for illegal charges if you notify the credit-card company immediately after losing your card. If you don't know about the loss for a while, however, then you are responsible. For example, one man we know was on an extended business trip during which time several credit cards were stolen from his home. On his return a stack of charges from credit-card companies awaited him. The thief had gone on a spree with his cards. The man was obligated to pay those charges, but the story had a happy ending. The man's insurance agent, knowing that he traveled considerably, had a short time before added credit-card coverage to the man's homeowners policy (which shows a good agent at work). The insurance company paid for the illegal charges.

INSURANCE SUMMED UP

The most expensive mistake to avoid is underinsuring a house. You save comparatively few dollars a year at the risk of losing a lot of money due to a fire or other big loss. Inflation in recent years puts special emphasis on keeping your insurance in line with the increased rebuilding costs for houses. Underinsurance on personal property and your household contents also should be avoided.

Most people will generally find that a homeowners HO-2 or HO-3 policy will be the best buy. You should also be sure to have satisfactory coverage for personal liability and for valuable possessions you may own. You may or may not need increased insurance over that given in the policy. For that matter, you may now have too much insurance, and you could save money by reducing it to a realistic level.

Do you have photographs of your house, both inside and outside? And an inventory and price records of personal property so you can substantiate the value of a future claim? If you can answer "yes" to these two questions and if you have reviewed and, if necessary, acted on the important points made in this chapter, your insurance should be in good shape. You may have to apply a little attention to your insurance now; it's one of those annoying chores which many of us tend to put off, but it makes plenty of sense not to do so. Putting your mind to it—merely calling your insurance man for a good review of your house insurance —may be all that you need do.

CHAPTER 8

HOME IMPROVEMENTS AND
REMODELING

▮ *How much typical home improvements cost . . . Finding a good
contractor . . . How to tell if the price is fair . . . Buying home-
improvement work and what to specify in your agreement . . .
Fixed-price and cost-plus contracts . . . Ways to save money . . .
Pitfalls to avoid . . . Financing home improvements at the
lowest interest rate . . . Eight kinds of home-improvement
loans . . . How much does remodeling increase the value of
your house? . . . Which improvements add the most to your
house and which add little or no value . . . Overimproving a
house . . . Avoiding the most common home-improvement
rackets.*

REMODELING A house can mean a comparatively simple thing like
installing new wiring or buying storm windows, or it may be a
major job like modernizing a kitchen or bath or adding a new
room or two to your house. A lot of money could be at stake. In
addition, the quality of the job—the workmanship—is also important unless you don't care about getting a good job properly
done with no problems left over.

The ideal way to get such work done is to come into a windfall
equal to about twice the cost of the improvement. Put the work
into the hands of a top-notch man whom you can count on, and
pay whatever the price is to get it all done right. With the other
half of the money take your family off to the Caribbean or Europe
until the work is finished. You've not only avoided the inevitable
frustrations and problems that can arise when construction is done
on a house, but you've had a great time away while it was being
done. If you can swing it, there's no need to read the rest of this
chapter.

If you cannot, then you would do well to arm yourself with a little knowledge about getting home improvements done properly and surviving. This includes how to spot a good contractor, paying a fair price, and, among other things, how to avoid common pitfalls that arise time after time. Here is what you should know about these and other facets of the subject when you must fix up, remodel, or modernize your house.

HOW MUCH MONEY WILL IT COST?

Naturally, the price will vary according to the type of work done. It will also vary according to who does the job, the quality of materials used, and how you buy the job. One couple we know had a new room added to their house. They were surprised and dismayed later when they heard that a neighbor down the street in a similar house had a new room added for $850 less than they paid. They wondered if they had been taken. Not so, it turned out. They had ordered special features, including built-in furniture and Thermopane windows, and their new room was also three feet longer—so no wonder they paid more. No two jobs, however seemingly alike, are likely to cost the same. Besides special materials and an extra feature or so for one job but not for the other, no two contractors are likely to bid the same price for the same work. Their bids may be close at times and far apart at other times.

This brings up one of the first basic rules: Always get at least two or three bids for new work. Don't necessarily take the lowest bid, though. As we've noted elsewhere, the low bid could be based on low quality, an incomplete job, or a contractor on the verge of bankruptcy who will do anything to get work. It's often a good idea, in fact, to discard an extremely low or extremely high bid and concentrate on the middle ones.

Know how contractors function. When business is slow and a man needs work, he often will bid low, allowing himself a small margin for profit. He wants and needs work, especially if it's necessary to keep his men busy. A busy contractor, on the other hand, may be so loaded with work that he couldn't care less about your job. He may indicate as much, never returning your calls, or he will put in an exceptionally, if not outrageously, high bid. At the moment he cares little about new work, and if he is going to take on more, it will only be at a high price and a really fat profit to make it worth his while. You generally can tell this only when you get more than one bid, and the extremely high man sticks out like a smokestack.

There are also, to be sure, contractors and dealers whose pricing is fairly uniform. These generally include the more secure and established men who have been around for a while. They're experienced and know how to estimate, and they generally add a standard markup for their overhead and profit. Their prices usually fall in the middle range.

What Do Typical Home Improvements Cost?

Know about how much money you must spend and, among other things, you'll be better able to tell when a quoted price is out of line. A little shopping around and asking questions will help here. Talk to families who've had similar work done. Become familiar with the reasons that the cost of your work may be higher or lower than usual.

Here are the average range of prices for common home improvements and some reasons that the price for a particular job can vary greatly, depending on unavoidable variables from house to house. The prices given are from a 1970 survey of home-improvement contractors in various parts of the country. As a result, they also reflect differences in such things as labor rates from one part of the country to another.

Remodeled kitchen. $1,750 to about $4,000 installed. Prices average approximately $100 per linear foot of new cabinets, countertop, and appliances but little or nothing else. The price

A simple kitchen can be highly attractive and low in cost. Open shelves (right) reduce cost of cabinets and also give convenient access to dishes.

This kitchen may at first glance look nice, but it's overdone and poorly designed. The fancy cabinet decorations are too much and could, among other things, reduce the sales appeal of the house if and when it is put up for sale. Also, the sink and range should be switched with each other for more efficient food preparation and cooking.

goes up if you install new flooring and walls, a new window or two, and if structural changes or alterations are needed. A large and elaborate new kitchen can cost $5,000 or more, especially if major structural changes are required.

New half-bath. $750 to $1,500. It will be on the low side if it is installed within an enclosed existing space (such as a closet converted to a half-bath) and if the plumbing connections are short and simple. The cost goes up if new partitions or long plumbing connections are required. The new fixtures, accessories, and materials account for about half of the cost and labor for the rest.

Remodeled full bath. $1,350 to $3,000, depending mainly on the fixtures and accessories desired. The price will be higher if new flooring and wall surfaces are put in. A complete new bathroom within an existing space will cost more because of the new plumbing hookup needed.

New attic room. About $1,250 to $3,000, depending on its size and whether a new roof dormer is needed. It will be on the low side for a moderate-size new room if there is adequate head room to start with in the attic, and a new dormer is not required. The price will generally get you a finished floor, walls and ceiling, insulation, wiring, and heating. If a new dormer is required, add approximately $100 to $125 a running foot, or $750 to $2,500.

Basement recreation room. $1,500 to $3,000, depending on the size and special work desired. It's on the low side for a small- to moderate-size room with new flooring, walls, ceiling, staircase, wiring, and lighting. The cost goes up for a larger room, especially if you need new partitions and if old pipes and ducts must be covered up.

New room added onto your house. About $12 to $20 per square foot of area for frame construction, up to $25 for masonry. That's for new living space, such as a family room or bedroom wing, including new foundations, walls and roof, heat and wiring, but not necessarily new plumbing. The exact price depends most on local building costs and whether or not special features are included.

Central air-conditioning. $900 to $1,500, installed, for adding a two- to three-ton cooling system to adequate existing warm-air

One new, compartmented bath can do double duty, especially during the morning rush hour. Two lavatories, like a two-lane highway, can handle a double load. The walled-off shower-toilet section gives third-person privacy. There's plenty of storage space, too. BETTER HOMES & GARDENS.

New packaged bathrooms like this can sharply reduce the cost of a new bathroom. The complete factory-made package comes in sections that will pass through a thirty-inch-wide doorway. They are connected together as shown. The pipes are connected to the house plumbing, and the exterior walls are closed in with any type of finished wall material you desire. The bathroom unit comes in different sizes and costs from about $1,000 to $1,250 plus installation cost. It's made by the Crane Company, 4100 S. Kedzie Ave., Chicago, Illinois 60632.

cutaway view of a Crane bathroom ows the interior fixtures and how the ctions are made. BETTER HOMES & RDENS.

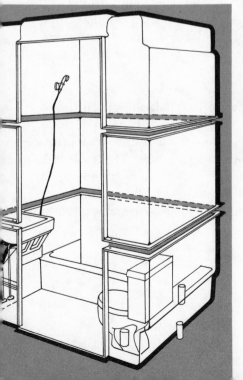

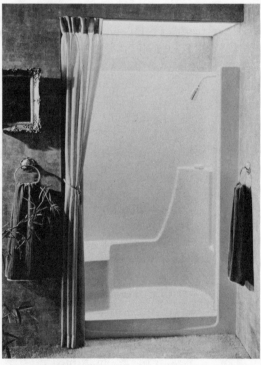

New fiber glass–reinforced shower stalls can simplify the installation and lower the cost of a custom bathroom. Various shapes and designs are available. OWENS-CORNING FIBERGLAS.

heating ducts in a house. The cost goes up for more cooling capacity—about $400 to $500, more or less, per additional ton of capacity, and more if new ductwork or wiring capacity is needed.

Air conditioning with room units. $150 to $325 per unit installed, depending on the unit size and the amount of new wiring needed. At least three to four units are generally required to cool all or most of the house.

New heating plant. $750 to $1,350 for a new warm-air furnace or heating boiler to replace a worn-out old one. Exact price depends on the capacity required and the amount of hookup labor needed. The price will be higher for a large house or if new ductwork or piping is needed.

Combination storm doors and windows. $20 to $40 each, installed, for average-size combination storm windows and screens. Prices are lowest for low-quality aluminum units, highest for the top-quality aluminum, steel, or rigid vinyl windows.

Storm doors cost about $75 to $110, installed, for the best-quality combination doors. Prices for fancy decorative doors of high-quality metal range up to about $150; the extra cost is almost entirely for the decorative design.

Aluminum siding. $80 to $110 per "square" (100 square feet of wall), installed. Top-quality insulating siding costs 10 to 15 per cent more than the standard noninsulating kind. The cost goes up for a house with a complicated shape, for varied windows that require more cutting and fitting, and for such extras as new aluminum soffit covers. The price for an average-size house ordinarily runs between $750 and $1,500.

New roofing. $25 to $40 per square (100 square feet of roof) for new, standard-weight (235-pound) asphalt shingles installed over your old roofing. Thus the price can vary from as little as $300, more or less, for a small house with a simple roof up to $1,250, and sometimes more, for a large house. The cost rises if your old roofing must be stripped off first; if there are a number of gables, hips, and other such breaks; if new flashing is required; or if a more expensive roofing material such as cedar shakes or asbestos cement is used.

Electrical work. $150 to $300 for a new 220-volt, 100- to 200-ampere electrical service. New wiring for an existing house averages about $8 to $15 for each new outlet or switch and $25 to $75 for each special circuit for, say, an electric dryer or air-conditioner. The heavier the wire and the longer the run needed, the greater the cost.

Wall paneling. 20¢ to 80¢ a square foot, excluding installation, for most common types, or about $8 to $25 per standard 4-by-8-foot sheet. The price is in the low to medium range for softwood, gypsum board, hardboard, and the most common plywood paneling. Better quality and more attractive plywoods, especially those with a hand-rubbed effect, and plastic laminate paneling are at the high level. The most handsome and exotic kinds of plywood and the prized hardwoods such as walnut, oak, and cherry can range from $1 to $3 a square foot.

New one-car carport or garage. $1,000 to $1,750 for carport; $1,500 to $3,500 for a new garage. Cost is lowest for the simplest frame construction and flat roof; higher for masonry walls and built-up roofing; highest with special features, such as built-in storage cabinets.

Exterior painting. Between $500 and $1,250 for most typical houses. Cost for a two-coat job can run 10¢ to 20¢ per square foot. The price varies according to how much cleaning and preparation the walls require before painting and the amount of woodwork to be painted. Cost is highest when old paint is in poor condition and must be scraped and removed prior to repainting. Incidentally, the very best paint is the cheapest paint in the long run. You may have to pay, say, $8 a gallon for top-quality paint versus $5 to $6 a gallon for the cheapest, but try to save a few dollars on the cheap paint and you'll probably have to repaint in a few years.

FINDING A GOOD CONTRACTOR

It's not always easy to find a good contractor. It may take a little time, but the few hours or even a day or so expended on finding a good man is virtually nothing compared with the loss in time

(measured in weeks and even months), money, and headaches
you may otherwise suffer trying to repair the damage wrought
by a man who botched up your house.

If you don't know of a good contractor or two, ask friends, relatives, and neighbors for the names of men who did good work for
them. Call the local Chamber of Commerce, which will sometimes recommend contractors. In a pinch, call a few local lumber
yards or wholesale suppliers (the people at an electrical- or
plumbing-supply house) who sell materials to contractors and
who generally know which contractors are good. The home-im-
provement-loan manager at a bank might recommend a man
or two. Check the yellow pages of your telephone book under
the contractor listing you want, though if you get a man cold
this way, check his credentials carefully before using him.

Before buying from a contractor, visit his showroom or office.
This will give you an idea of whether he's in business for good
or not. For that matter, does he have an office? Some perfectly
good men operate out of their homes, which is all right too, but
then go a step farther and call a few people he's done work for,
particularly before letting him tackle a really big job on your
house. A man who will not or cannot give you names of people
he's worked for should be held suspect on that score alone.

How long has he been in business locally? What about a few
financial references?—his bank, for example. Be sure he has insurance (to protect you from a liability suit for a nasty injury on
the job to one of his workmen or anybody else). He should have
Workman's Compensation and property-damage and liability insurance. An established contractor has such insurance. He will
gladly show you proof or give you the name of his insurance
broker, whom you may call.

Is His Price Fair?

Again, the best way to tell if a price is reasonable is to get at
least two or three bids. Also let the contractor know that you're
getting other bids. He'll usually sharpen his pencil and avoid

the tendency to inflate his price. You may never hear from some men again, but that's usually because they realize they can't gouge you, and then they don't want the work.

Compare each bid to be sure that each contractor is bidding on the same basis. An extremely low bid may be explained by the fact that something has been omitted from the job. An extremely high bid could indicate a job padded with unnecessary frills and extras.

The contract may be either a firm contract at a stipulated price or one with a cost-plus agreement. Let's look at both types.

The Firm-Price Contract

Putting your firm-price contract in writing will avoid unpleasantness and those unexpected extras that sometimes get tacked on at the end, making your total price for the job balloon. A good man ordinarily, though not always, gives you a written proposal. Read it, and if you don't make at least one change, there's something wrong.

Include a clause in the contract that allows you to withhold at least 10 to 20 per cent of the final payment until the job is completed to your satisfaction. Some contractors have a frustrating habit of finishing nearly everything and then vanishing for a month or two, leaving you amid the debris. This is less likely if the man still has money due from you. Such delays are sometimes unavoidable because the man has unexpected trouble with his lumber deliveries or his men have taken off on him because the hunting season has started. Give the man some leeway, but don't be a patsy. The partial payment withheld by you will get the man back to complete the work as soon as possible.

Insert a completion date in the contract saying that the work is to be done by a certain date. If it is not, this clause should spell out your right to bring in another contractor to finish the job up, with the price charged to the original man's contract price. Be flexible on the date, but do protect yourself.

A sketch, drawing, or plan of the work, if applicable, should be put on the contract. If necessary, you draw the sketch; it need not be an architectural masterpiece. A list of the materials to be provided, including brand names and specific equipment clearly identified, should be included. Sometimes the specific thing you've contracted for may be unobtainable, and then the contractor must substitute. You're protected if the agreement says that he is to provide the Great Day Swidget, Model A, "or the equivalent."

Be fair and reasonable, and the contractor will be encouraged to be the same way with you. If you have questions, this is the time to raise them. If necessary, put the answers in the contract so there's no question later. People have short memories during times of conflict, and it's easy to forget a verbal agreement over which way the walls were to be done or how the pipes were to run.

The Cost-Plus Contract

The cost-plus contract is used chiefly when the nature of a job makes it difficult if not impossible to estimate the work accurately. An old wall or two may have to come down, and no one can tell how much work it will require, not to mention what might be discovered inside that could complicate things.

Again the cardinal rule is: Get it in writing. Draw up an agreement as just outlined for a firm-price contract except that no stipulated price is included. Instead you are charged according to the contractor's cost for materials and labor plus a 10 to 20 per cent markup. Fifteen per cent is a good compromise. Ten is a borderline price that might barely cover a man's overhead and tempt him to cut a corner or two. Twenty per cent can be good if you're feeling generous and if you wish to give the man breathing room and extra incentive to do a good job for you.

A cost-plus contract also can be an invitation for a man to toss in everything but the kitchen sink (even that sometimes), knowing that everything for the job is marked up. That's a potential danger you can avoid in the following way. First, the contractor should give you an approximate total price estimate for the job. Second, he should present you with a list of all materials used when he bills you, with the cost of each backed up by a copy of his bills from suppliers. A contractor almost always gets a trade discount on his materials, and this can sometimes be substantially less than the list price. Your contract should specify that you will pay his actual cost plus the agreed-upon markup. His price to you therefore should be based on his net cost for materials.

The hourly price for labor on the job also should be in the agreement. This means his per-hour cost for his carpenters, mechanics, and other workers and should include the fringe expenses that the contractor pays each man for social security, union dues, and so on, on top of each worker's hourly price-scale.

If you have not had work done on your house in the past few years, be prepared for a jolt. In quite a few places plumbers, electricians, and other skilled men now get eight dollars to ten dollars an hour, if not more. Anything you can do to cut down the hours of labor will save you a pretty penny. This goes for a firm-price agreement, as well as for the cost-plus contract.

By and large, the firm price is the better way. Reserve the cost-plus method only for a job that really cannot be pinned down and estimated beforehand.

Work Changes

If you change your mind midway through a job, you should expect to pay more. The smallest-seeming change can require a great deal of changing gears and revamping the job plan and thus involve a higher cost for the contractor. Some changes, to be sure, may cut his work, and then you should get a credit. Whatever the change is, it too should be put in writing at the time, with the extra price you will pay for it. If you do not do so, don't be surprised if you are later presented with a major bill for what you thought was a trivial change.

SAVING MONEY ON HOME IMPROVEMENTS

There are various ways to save money on home improvements, but they may require a little time and effort on your part.

Do a little homework and hard thinking before starting a job. What exactly is the real purpose of the remodeling or improvement planned? Can you fulfill your primary objective without doing everything you originally thought was necessary? Discuss the work in detail with contractors. Ask them what you might do to cut down the extent of the job and the amount of work that they must do.

An architect might save you money, particularly on a major remodeling job. He could give you good suggestions and then draw a plan for the contractors to follow. You pay him a stipulated fee, sometimes based on an hourly charge for his time. This could greatly simplify things for a contractor and also mean that every contractor bids on the same specifications. Most of all, a good architect, like a good doctor or lawyer, can bring much experience to bear on a major job which will more than save you the cost of his fee. An architect, however, is not usually required for such work as new heating, wiring, painting, and other such one-stop work. He can serve best for new construction or living space added to a house and also be helpful on a consulting basis for a new kitchen or bathroom.

Try to determine the major cost items for the work. We've already noted that a new dormer, for example, can be a major cost item when an attic is converted into living space. Is it really needed? Can it be eliminated (by installing skylight windows, say, rather than conventional new windows)?

What about the materials used? Can you omit some of those expensive items and substitute lower-priced but equally good materials? Consider, for example, fixed-glass windows here or there, especially if you have air conditioning. They're about half the cost of conventional windows. Or could you do the job in a different way? Think through the whole job, and often you'll be amazed at how much can be saved by applying a little imagination and ingenuity to your plan.

Perhaps you can do some of the work yourself. Hire a contractor to do the serious part of the work which requires skilled professionals, such as the foundation, structural shell, and roof

Use imagination. A new window like this one can vastly improve a house without major alterations and at a comparatively low cost. PONDEROSA PINE WOODWORK.

of a new addition. Depending on your personal skill and inclination, a do-it-yourself man or man-and-wife team might put down the finished floor tile, apply trim and woodwork, and paint the job. Discuss this with contractors. Often they'll be delighted to provide only the main part of the work and let you finish up. But put this clearly in your written agreement.

Should you be your own contractor? You'll need special stamina and patience to ride herd on subcontractors and cope with the necessary scheduling. Then you might save about 10 to 20 per cent of the total price that a complete job handled by an overall contractor would otherwise cost. You could save up to four hundred dollars on a new bathroom or family room for which a contractor would charge two thousand dollars. You must run the show, however, individually hiring the necessary carpenters, plumbers, electricians, and other tradesmen required for each

Don't be afraid of breaking with tradition. This large window is made with insulating glass and cost less than two hundred dollars, installed, chiefly because it uses fixed glass. There's no need to open it because of air conditioning. It transformed the room, as you can see from the "before" picture of the small window formerly in the same room.

part of the work. Some jobs, such as a new addition, can require as many as a dozen or so subcontractors, including a mason, excavation man, spackler, and roofer, as well as carpenters, electricians, and heating man. It's best, however, to hire a single home-improvement contractor to do a big job like that.

A smaller job that may require no more than three or four different tradesmen is obviously easier to contract out yourself. This could be a new bathroom, possibly a simple new kitchen, or an interior conversion. New heating, wiring, roofing, and that kind of work generally requires only one trade for which you automatically serve as your own contractor.

If you act as your own contractor, have a written agreement with every man you hire. Follow the guidelines given earlier in this chapter. Draw up plans and specifications, and leave nothing to unwritten chance. You'll have to arrange for the building permit, if required, and possibly take out temporary contractor's insurance.

Being your own contractor is no cinch. Do it only if you've had a little experience and only if you're willing to expend the time and effort to do it right.

ZONING RULES AND BUILDING CODES

We know of a man who added a wing to the side of his house at no small expense, and then the sheriff showed up and told him to tear it down. There were no ifs, ands, or buts about it. The man had violated the local zoning law that prohibited new construction that close to the side of his building lot. He had to spend more money to tear down the new addition.

This points up the importance of checking your local zoning before you launch into new work on your house. You must also adhere to the local building code. A good architect or contractor will usually handle such requirements when he submits a plan for your building permit. It's a good idea, though, to check yourself that your job conforms with the local zoning law.

FINANCING HOME IMPROVEMENTS

You can borrow money to fix up your house at a mere 4 to 5 per cent straight, simple interest rate up to as much as 20 to 25 per cent interest. There is no standard charge for such loans, just as there is no standard price for a particular improvement.

Here are eight different ways to finance a remodeling job. You can, by the way, often borrow money in the same way for other purposes, such as getting the bundle of cash to send a child to college. There are usually no strings attached to what you do with the money except for the F.H.A. loan noted. The charge noted here for each loan is the true annual rate of interest.

1. *Life-insurance loan,* 4 to 6 per cent per year simple interest.

You borrow against the cash value that has built up in a permanent life-insurance policy. The interest charge is noted in the policy. You pay the loan back at any time. That's a great inducement, and the cost is small, but there's also the human tendency to put off repaying this loan. If you do not pay it off, new interest is added to your premium each year. If the insurance policy is cashed in or paid to a beneficiary, the unpaid amount of the loan is deducted from the insurance payment.

2. *Bank-collateral loan,* 5 to 8 percent interest, depending on the cost of money and national interest rates at the time. You often can get one for as short a period as ninety days or up to a year or more. You must have a good credit rating and generally you must put up collateral such as stocks and bonds or the title to any real estate you may own. It's a cheap loan if you qualify. That's because the bank takes virtually no risk. If the loan isn't paid, your collateral is used to repay it.

3. *Refinancing your house mortgage,* 5 to perhaps 9 per cent interest, depending on current mortgage costs. In effect, you turn in your present mortgage for a new one that is increased by the new sum of money you borrow. Say your present mortgage has a balance of fourteen thousand dollars, and you need five thousand dollars to fix up your house. You exchange your present mortgage for a new mortgage, promising to pay back the bank nineteen thousand dollars, and it gives you five thousand dollars in cash to pay for the work.

This is recommended, however, only when you must borrow at least three thousand to four thousand dollars or more. That's because you must generally pay new closing costs and other such charges to swing the deal, just as when you got the mortgage in the first place. If less money is needed, you'll generally do better to borrow it with an installment loan at a higher interest rate but no extra closing-cost charges, as noted below. Your closing-cost charges could be low, however, if you have an "open-end" clause in your present mortgage. If you do, it means, in effect, that you can refinance your mortgage without a lot of fuss and legal bother. Read the mortgage, or call the bank to find out. With it, the cost of refinancing your mortgage will be minimal.

The interest rate on a new, refinanced mortgage is generally based on the prevailing interest charged for mortgages at the time you borrow. Sometimes it stays the same on your original mortgage balance and goes up only for the new money borrowed. If the interest rate will go up sharply on the whole new mortgage, refinancing it may not be so cheap. It may not be a good idea.

4. *F.H.A. home-improvement loan,* 8.8 to 10.8 per cent interest. This is the cheapest regular home-improvement loan. You get one from a bank, or credit union, and sometimes from the home-improvement dealer selling you a job. It's arranged easily. The loan is actually made by a private lender and not the Government (which only guarantees the lender against loss). An F.H.A. home-improvement loan can be had for up to five thousand dollars, though this limit may be changed. Information can be had from any F.H.A. office, or write the Federal Housing Administration, Washington, D.C. 20140.

5. *A credit-union loan,* about 9 to 12 per cent interest. Get it from a credit union you belong to at work or as a member of a social or professional group. It's a straight installment loan made the way a bank does it, but it's usually cheaper. Take this loan only if your credit union cannot give you an F.H.A. loan (which could save you a few dollars).

6. *Bank's "own loan,"* about 10 to 16 per cent interest. It's the standard personal or installment loan made by banks, like those given to buy a car, appliance, or furniture. The interest rate can vary from bank to bank, so shopping a few banks could save you money.

7. *Dealer-installment loan,* about 12 to 20 per cent interest. This is generally what you get when you finance the job through the home-improvement dealer who sells you the job. He's a middleman, handling the loan for a bank or finance company with whom he has an arrangement. The credit charge will vary according to the particular lender he does business with. Some-

times the credit charge you pay includes a "commission" for the dealer, and you pay more. An F.H.A. home-improvement loan from a dealer can be a good, low-cost loan, since its rate is fixed by law. Otherwise, you will generally save by arranging your own financing.

8. *Finance-company loan,* about 15 to 25 per cent interest. Its cost is usually highest of all. It's therefore recommended only if you really need the money and can't borrow anywhere else. The rates are high because a finance company will lend to virtually all comers and therefore risks the most on its loans. A finance company, of course, is a money lender, a company whose business is to make loans.

How Much Interest Are You Paying?

What are you actually being charged for interest? And is an additional credit charge or loan fee tacked on to the money you must pay back? These are good questions to ask and answer before you borrow money. Figure up the total interest and other charges you must pay on a particular loan, and the sum might set your mind at ease—or shock you.

It's easily done. You merely multiply the monthly installment to be repaid by the number of installments to be made. Subtract from that the sum of money borrowed. Say you need a $1,000 loan for your house, for a new roof, for example. It's to be repaid in twelve monthly installments of $87.72 each. Multiply 12 by $87.72, and you get $1,052.64. That's the total amount you pay for a $1,000 loan. The interest is $52.64 ($1,052.64 minus $1,000).

Those are actual figures for a $1,000 F.H.A. home-improvement loan to be repaid in a year. The true annual interest on that same loan is 10.8 per cent. It's not 5.264 per cent, even though it may seem to be that for a one-year loan, because as the loan is partly repaid, each month the balance owed diminishes in successive steps. Over the whole year the average money out on loan to you is only about half the total, or about $500. Since you pay an interest charge of some $53 to borrow that much money on average for a year, your true interest is just over twice the apparent percentage, or 10.8 per cent.

The true annual interest you pay on a loan must be disclosed to you when you borrow. It's usually noted on a loan form, though you might have to look for it in the fine print. Also check for other charges and fees you may have to pay, such as a charge for credit life-insurance (to pay back the borrower in case the lender dies).

HOW MUCH DO HOME IMPROVEMENTS INCREASE THE VALUE OF YOUR HOUSE?

You might save a good deal of money by not spending it on a big deal for your house just because you hope to sell your house at a higher price. With a few exceptions, that seldom pays. Money should be spent on a house chiefly for the pleasure and benefits for you and your family while you're living in it.

A new kitchen, new bath or half-bath, and a third or fourth bedroom are the features most sought after by home buyers and are therefore the ones that most increase the value of a house. The value of a house will go up as much as 75 to 100 per cent of the cost of such improvements. That assumes that you don't go overboard on the improvement and that it is right for your house. You don't, for example, put a five-thousand-dollar kitchen in a fifteen-thousand-dollar house; it's obviously too much.

A new family room, again assuming it's well done, should increase house value by about 50 to 75 per cent of its cost. A new garage or carport will pay off if it's the customary car shelter for your climate. A garage is obviously more desirable in a cold climate, whereas a carport is all right in a warmer climate such as southern California. A screened porch, breezeway, or "Florida room" are highly desirable in the South but less so in the North. Thus the money invested in such geographically affected improvements will be reflected in a higher house value depending on where you live.

A swimming pool and central air-conditioning are growing in desirability throughout many parts of the North as well as the South. Money spent on each of them is increasingly reflected in higher resale value of a house, though this is not always so. They will generally increase the value of a house by about 50 per cent of their cost and sometimes even up to 75 per cent or more. A swimming pool, however, will generally not increase the value of a house by more than about 15 per cent, more or less, of the house value before the pool.

A new basement recreation-room, paneled den, elaborate built-in furniture, and special landscaping and gardening will increase house value the least, no matter how much money you put into such features. As a rule, home buyers don't consider them essential and therefore will not pay extra for them. One Connecticut man, an outdoor greenery lover, put more than ten thousand dollars into landscaping his house. He was crushed later to learn that he would not get it back when he sold his house. Real-estate appraisers increased the value of the house by very little because of the extensive landscaping. They were right. No potential buyer would pay that much more for the house just because of the elaborate (and quite lovely) landscaping.

A new roof, new heating furnace, and other "maintenance" improvements also do not increase the value of a house by much. These are nonetheless essential. They are recommended when you need such repairs, because they preserve the value of your house. Without such repairs a house will run down in value. In short, they maintain the value of a house.

About the only money you should spend on a house to sell it at a higher price is for repairs that are obviously needed to put your best foot forward when you put the house on the market. This can include repainting the outside, one of the very few large expenditures that can make a big difference when you sell. (More on selling a house in Chapter 10.)

We repeat: Fix up and improve a house chiefly for your own

pleasure and satisfaction. By and large, don't spend money on an investment calculated only to increase a house's resale value. Besides, the improvements that are done with a true belief in their value for one's own family use are generally those that are most likely to boost the value of the house the most.

Don't Over-improve

All bets are off if you overvalue your house in relation to other houses in the neighborhood. An old real-estate axiom says, in effect, that nobody will spend $40,000 for a house in a $30,000 neighborhood. That's virtually true regardless of how large and good a house it may be.

One young couple in downstate Illinois spent $12,000 for improvements on a forty-year-old house they had bought for $18,000. The husband was suddenly transferred across the country, and they put the house up for sale at $30,000, the sum they had invested in it. Nobody would buy it because it was in a neighborhood of $20,000 to $25,000 houses. They finally had to sell for $24,500, taking a beating to the tune of $5,500.

That was the most they could get. People with more money to spend on a house wanted to live in a neighborhood of $30,000-and-up houses. In short, the top value of other houses around should be approximately the top value you can expect to get for your house and therefore the ceiling on the money you invest in your house.

That's assuming that you will sell and move someday and want to get all your money out of your house. You can break that rule, however, if you dearly love your house and if the economics of ownership are less important to you than having a splendid house to live in. You may not expect to move for a long time; then by all means remodel and fix up without rigid adherence to the over-improvement peril. You'll get your investment back in increased living benefits from your house over the years. And if you live in an area of rising home values, you may not lose out much at all. Other people around may also be improving their houses, so the overall value of the neighborhood is on the rise.

AVOIDING THE HOME-IMPROVEMENTS GYP

It could never happen to me, you may say. These are famous last words. Not long ago, for example, a newspaper reported the sad tale of a woman who had been taken by a contractor. She and her husband hired the man to do a $3,500 remodeling job, which they were borrowing money to pay for. Halfway through the work the contractor asked a favor. He was short of money for the materials needed to finish the job. Would she mind signing the loan completion slip so he could get paid by the bank and finish the work. She could count on him, he said. Sorry for the man, the woman signed the loan paper saying that the job was completed. The contractor was paid in full by the bank and was never heard from again. The woman and her husband nonetheless were responsible for paying back the full amount of the loan. They also had to borrow more to get another contractor to finish the job.

That has happened more than once. The specific lesson to learn is: Never sign a completion paper until your job *is* completely and totally done. Some of the worst of the contractors' breed will surreptitiously try to get homeowners to sign the completion end of the job contract or a loan paper right in the beginning when they get the order. "Just sign here and there," such men will say. Second lesson: Read before you sign, no matter how friendly and trustworthy a salesman appears to be.

The number of crooks and gyps in the home-improvement field may be no greater than in other fields, though at times it does seem to be infested with crooks. Probably the worst are itinerants who travel from town to town and solicit from door to door. They have no permanent local office or showroom.

So lesson number three: Don't buy from anyone, especially from a doorbell salesman, without checking on him.

Certain ploys and slick tricks of the trade are commonly used by dishonest salesmen and dealers. By and large, these are made to sound like an irresistible bargain, something you simply cannot afford to pass up. Three notorious selling methods, often used with great and disarming slickness, are the "model-home" ploy, the "bait-and-switch" advertisement, and "low balling."

The model-home ploy, also called the referral racket, has a salesman telling you that he can give you a big break on his price because he wants to use your installation as a model for other people to see. He may be selling aluminum siding, a new roof, a built-in vacuum system—you name it. "What's more, it really won't cost you a cent," he says. "For every person referred to us as a result of seeing your installation, we'll pay you fifty dollars—how's that? Surely you know at least a dozen people right away. You'll be making money!" he adds, full of enthusiasm. "All you do is sign here. You'll get our special discount price to start with, and your money starts flowing back as soon as the job is complete!"

The homeowner signs up, gets the product, and that's the last time he ever sees the man. What's more, if he checks, he will also find that the "special discount price" is higher than the standard price charged. So when a salesman mentions using your house as a model home, beware, especially if he promises to pay you for every prospect you turn over to him later.

A "bait-and-switch" advertisement also holds alluring appeal. It offers a major home-improvement or product at an irresistibly low price. It may be aluminum storm windows at "an unbeatable $18.95 each," "a complete new kitchen for $795!," or a "new stone front for a 30-foot house for only $149!" Answer one of the ads —made on the radio or TV as well as in print—and you'll be told that the item advertised is all sold out. "Besides," a salesman will add, "those storm windows were really trash. Now here are top-notch windows that just came in—the very best. We've only got a small quantity left, but you can have them for thirty-nine fifty apiece. They can't be beat!" You're baited by a low price and switched to an outrageous price for a product that is hardly any better.

The stone-front ploy is an attempt to get you to buy "really genuine stone" for $1,295. The kitchen come-on will get you a delivery of a few kitchen cabinets, dropped on your front porch, but then there's an extra charge, perhaps $1,000 or more, to install the cabinets. Once you see them, however, you'd rather you never saw them again.

"Low balling" operates on the same principle. You may be offered an irresistibly low price for some construction work such as a new attic bedroom. After you order the job, however, the contractor will do a little work and stop. He's all finished, he'll say, though the flooring, wallboard, and a few other things are still lacking. "Oh, that wasn't in the price," he'll say. To complete the job will require another $1,500. You look at the original order and, sure enough, it says nothing about things like finished flooring and walls.

To avoid this, be sure to check the agreement ahead of time. It's amazing how often people sign papers without reading them. "Oh, it's all there," the salesman will assure you. "No need to read all that legal gobbledygook." Some salesmen, as a matter of fact, can be relied on, but you can't tell which until later. To play it safe, read before you sign.

The home-improvement field is not really a jungle of man-eating tigers out to get the homeowner at any cost, but a number of slick crooks do operate in the field. Fixing up an existing house, adding to it, or carrying out other kinds of improvement work can, because of the nature of such work, be difficult and complicated, but this should not frighten you. We have discussed some of the worst things that could happen chiefly to emphasize the importance of planning a job properly and taking the time to check on a contractor beforehand. In short, use only the best men around.

What about specific things to know about specific kinds of home-improvement jobs? What should you know when you need a new kitchen or bathroom? When you're adding a new room, rewiring, or buying a new water heater or furnace? Books have been written on these subjects. Borrow a good one from the library. Some may be superficial, but others can be of great help. One such book we recommend (since it was written by the author of this book) is *The Complete Book of Home Remodeling, Improvement, and Repair,* available in some libraries, or you can buy a paperback copy for $1.45. If unavailable locally, send $1.45 plus 35¢ for postage and handling to All About Houses, 855 River Road, Piermont, New York 10968.

■ *Clues that lead burglars to a house . . . Basic safeguards that
fend off thieves and reduce the likelihood of burglary . . .
Avoiding common mistakes that make houses vulnerable . . .
What to do when you leave home for a time . . . Door and
window locks . . . Alarm systems . . . Safes . . . How a thief
burglarizes a house . . . Choosing a watchdog . . . Special tips.*

NOT LONG ago a lady got in her car at 9:30 one morning and
drove off on a round of errands. She locked the front door of
her house, of course, but left the garage door open as she drove
off. About ten minutes later a car entered the driveway, and two
men in work clothes got out. They casually went to the rear
door, jimmied it, and entered the house. Within ten minutes they
had looted the house of $8,000 worth of property, including a
color TV-set, golf clubs, two cameras, a fur coat, irreplaceable
heirlooms, jewelry (among which was the woman's prized necklace and two diamond rings), and some $350 in cash.

It was a typical home burglary. More than 1.5 million burglaries
now occur each year. It is the fastest growing crime in the
United States, according to the F.B.I. Household burglaries account for more than half of the total. A burglary is "unlawful
entry with intent to steal." Robbery is "the stealing or taking
of anything of value from a person by use of force or threat
of force."

At the current rate, about one hundred houses a day will be
burglarized this year, or about one every four minutes. The
largest number of burglaries occur on weekday mornings from
about 9:30 to 11 A.M. when a husband and children are off to
work and school and when evidence indicates that a wife has

193

left the house. An open garage door and the car gone often supplies the evidence. Some professional thieves will phone first to make sure no one is home. They get your phone number from your name on the mailbox, if necessary. (This has prompted police to recommend omitting your name from your curbside mailbox—just leave your street number on it.)

Home burglaries are increasing fastest in the suburbs, particularly in affluent neighborhoods. A typical professional thief will generally zero in on a particular neighborhood, rather than a particular house. He'll cruise the area during the day looking for likely house targets. Telltale signs of an unoccupied house which stir his adrenalin are mail or newspapers piled out front, uncut grass or unshoveled snow, or an empty garage. A decision is quickly made and the man, with or without an accomplice, will drive up and casually go to the door, looking for all the world as if he's making a legitimate call. A professional burglar can get into most houses and be off with the loot in an amazingly short time. He can, however, be shut out or at least delayed and partially stymied if you take a few precautions and use a little knowledge to prevent a burglary or theft.

"First-class" burglars account for a small minority of the total but are the toughest to keep out. Los Angeles County, California, an area with one of the highest burglary rates in the nation, harbors as many as ten thousand part-time burglars and house thieves, according to police estimates there. The police say, however, that only about one hundred of them are first-class thieves.

Most burglars steer clear of a house or apartment that's occupied. Breaking in and robbing the people inside carries a much heavier penalty than burglary (no force), which reduces the possibility of physical harm to the victim. There are dangerous intruders, to be sure. If someone stealthily enters your home at night and wakes you when you're asleep, give up whatever he will take as the price of your personal safety. If someone forces his way in during the day, experts have no perfect advice for foiling him. Some recommend passive subservience, not provoking him, as the best advice for preserving your physical safety. Better still, keep him out in the first place.

DON'T "INVITE" BURGLARS

Lock your doors and windows. An astonishing number of people do not. About one-third of all illegal entries into houses and apartments are made through an open door or window, according to police records. One New York City detective, shaking his head with disbelief, tells about checking an apartment house in a section of town where the tenants were clamoring for more crime protection. Routinely checking the building one morning, he found that the doors to six of the twenty apartments where no one was home were unlocked.

If you're going away for a while—on vacation, for example—ask a friend or neighbor to keep an eye on your house. Put your house on the police "empty-house" list, and they'll pay special attention to it. Arrange for your grass to be trimmed and stop mail and newspaper deliveries or arrange for them to be picked up by someone. In winter, arrange for snow to be shoveled off your sidewalk and driveway.

If you have a second car, leave it parked outside in full view. Remove the distributor cap to prevent its being stolen. Install a light timer, or photoelectric cell (about ten dollars to twenty dollars), that will turn an inside light on in the evening and automatically turn it off late at night. A couple of these in different parts of the house are best, particularly if they're set to go on and off at different times. You could also plug an electric radio into one of the timers to scare off a potential intruder.

Consider hiring a telephone-answering service to answer your phone while you're away, especially if your house is an inviting target. That's to mislead the thief who phones to see if anyone's home. Sometimes the telephone company will switch your incoming calls to a friend or neighbor if you're away for at least three or four weeks. Ask the telephone company about this.

Don't publicize the glorious news of your impending vacation trip, especially with an announcement on the society page of the local newspaper. Thieves not only read but the shrewd ones check the papers for such vital information. Save the social announcement till you return.

Don't leave notes outside for the milkman or any other deliveryman saying that nobody's home, even if you're going off just for an hour or so. One doctor left such a note on his front door, requesting a parcel service to leave an expected package next door, since he and his wife would be away till late that night. The parcel never came, but a thief did, looting the house at leisure to the tune of sixty thousand dollars' worth of jewelry, silver, and other valuables. The family was quite well off (at least before they were robbed).

Before leaving your house for an extended time, make a visual inspection from the street. Are there any signs that you're away? Pretend you're looking through the eyes of a burglar scanning the house as a target. The windows are likely to be shut, which is all right in winter, but not so in summer. Open a few on the second floor, and put in a screen to simulate occupancy. With a one-story house, use a small screen or two in windows that are secured to open only a few inches. A little rain might get in, but that can be handled by a bath mat on the floor inside. Besides notifying the police to put your house on their surveillance list, have a friend or neighbor come by to check things inside every few days (not only for safety, but also to catch a possible broken pipe or other such accident).

USE GOOD LOCKS

Even a run-of-the-mill thief can quickly open the usual housedoor lock or jimmy the door. A tough lock must be "picked," which takes more experience.

The usual lock has a spring mechanism that can be forced open by a strong, sharp twist of the knob, by a screwdriver, or by "loiding." A thief loids a door by slipping a piece of celluloid or a credit card between the door and its frame to push back the tongue of a snap lock. He can't do this, however, if you have

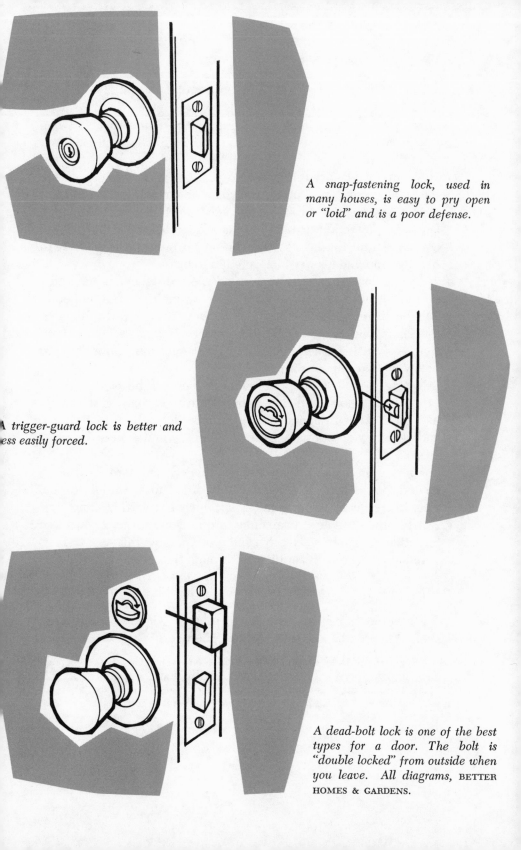

A snap-fastening lock, used in many houses, is easy to pry open or "loid" and is a poor defense.

A trigger-guard lock is better and less easily forced.

A dead-bolt lock is one of the best types for a door. The bolt is "double locked" from outside when you leave. All diagrams, BETTER HOMES & GARDENS.

a "dead-bolt" lock, the very minimum protection to have. It uses a bolt to lock the door, and you can see them in a hardware store. Get the kind that snaps into place automatically when you leave, rather than one that requires double-locking the door from the outside.

A pane of glass within reach of the lock in a door is another soft spot. A man can break the glass and reach in and release almost any lock that can be opened from the inside without a key. The protection needed here is a dead-bolt lock that is key-operated from the inside. You could also replace the glass with heavy, tempered glass, which is tough to break.

A chain lock adds extra security. Some are key-operated, which permits you to chain the door shut on retiring, but a family member coming home late at night can still get in by opening the chain with his key. It also permits you to lock the chain from the outside when you leave. This could fool a burglar into believing that someone is inside.

Nearly every key-operated cylinder lock can be picked by an expert, but a good one that is harder to pick than most can be had for from ten dollars to fifty dollars, depending on the lock and whether or not you can fit a new cylinder in your present lock.*

To prevent a door from being jimmied and forced open, a second lock is generally needed in addition to a dead-bolt lock. This usually calls for a Segal lock, which has vertical bolts and is made by a number of manufacturers. Don't forget good locks for other doors besides the front door. Many thieves, in fact, automatically go to a rear door or through the garage.

Windows

Metal blocks can be installed to prevent windows from being opened more than a few inches. There are also window bar

* Some of the locks recommended by the New York City Police Department include the Abloy, Chicago Ace Tubular, Eagle Supre Security (3-Star), Illinois Duo, Ingersoll, Medeco cylinder (usable with almost any lock you may have), Miracle Magnetic, and Sargent Keso.

grilles, especially recommended for apartment windows in a vulnerable neighborhood, and key-operated window locks. (Put the key within reach from inside but not where someone can reach it from outside.)

Double-hung windows can be secured quite easily with two ten-penny nails. Drill holes at a slight angle (down from inside to outside) through the upper rail of the bottom sash into the lower rail of the upper sash. Make the holes slightly larger than the nails, one on each side of the window. Then drop the nails in. Lift them out any time you want to open the window.

Watch Your Keys

Don't put one key outside under the door mat or around the corner of the house on a nail or any other obvious place. An amazing number of people do. Burglars often locate the key and enter with ease. Be original. Hide a backup key outside where nobody else will find it, at least fifteen to twenty feet from the door.

Don't distribute your keys freely among household help or friends and relatives. For obvious reasons don't put your name and address on a key ring. Remove the house key from the key ring when you leave your car and keys at a parking lot. Attendants have been known to duplicate the house key and pass it on with your license-plate number to a confederate. A thief then gets your address and with your key has entry to the house.

ALARM SYSTEMS

One kind of alarm system emits an ear-piercing siren; others set off loud bells, turn on the lights, or instantaneously notify police headquarters or a private police agency (like Holmes or Burns), which brings police on the double. Prices vary from as little as two dollars to five dollars for a battery-operated noise-maker wired to the front door up to several thousand dollars for an elaborate electronic police-notifying kind. Some are also fire alarms or incorporate urgency buttons that will bring help in case of an emergency, such as a heart attack.

An electronic system wired to your main doors and windows can cost from about $200 to $1,000—more for a very large house —depending on the number of doors and windows covered. The elaborate electronic system that brings police on the double can run as high as $2,500 to $5,000, again depending on the extent of coverage required.

The amount you spend should be determined, of course, by the value of your personal possessions and how much mental security you desire. By and large, the typical house will be reasonably well protected without an expensive alarm system if you have good locks on the doors and use the other ways to fend off a potential burglar described in this chapter. If your valuables consist of jewelry and other small items, a good safe may also be needed. If you live in a high-risk area, an alarm on each of your vulnerable windows and doors may suffice, coupled with good locks on each.

To determine the best alarm for your house, consult your local police chief. Ask him what other people nearby have and which kind works best locally. See what's listed in the classified pages of your telephone book. For information about the best, most elaborate electronic systems, consult such national burglar-alarm people as Holmes and Burns. Before buying any alarm system, however, check on the dealer carefully, since a number of dishonest people operate in the alarm field.

An alarm system has limitations, too. It can be expensive to wire all your doors and windows into the system, and some burglars have a sixth sense for sniffing out one of the few un-protected entries. An alarm system requires periodic attention, and you must remember to set it when you go out and turn it off when you return.

SAFES

A good safe is the place to keep jewelry, cash, negotiable se-curities, and valuable records. Get one with double walls and heat-resistant insulation that protect the contents against fire.

A safe should be solidly anchored because even the heaviest kind can be put on a dolly and carried off. It should be anchored to a wall or to the floor with bolts that cannot be easily cut with a hacksaw. The bolts will be saw-proof if they're set in place within a pipe that loosely encloses them. Attacked by a saw, the pipe will revolve, and the saw is stymied. A good safe can be had for as little as fifty dollars to one hundred dollars. The greater the value of the items in it, the more you should spend for a top-notch safe. And remember that anchoring a safe solidly can be as important as the type of safe used.

Put the safe in a good location. Don't put it in a side wall of a clothes closet where it's supposedly concealed by hanging clothes. That's one of the first places a burglar reaches for. Another place he goes right to is the wall behind a picture, particularly in the master bedroom. One of the best safes for a house is a round-door lug-type, solidly anchored in a closet floor, particularly if it's a concrete floor.

In addition to a safe, choose one closet for keeping expensive furs and other such items, and lock its door with a combination or Cypher lock (the kind used for classified areas in Government offices). It may not be impenetrable by the very best

A safe should be bolted to the house structure and have a combination lock. One with double-insulated walls will also protect contents from fire. HERCULES.

burglar, but it will often be safe from the usual hit-and-run sneak thief and run-of-the-mill intruder.

Combination locks that are pick-proof are generally the rule on safes, but all is lost if you hide the combination near the safe. A burglar has an eye for anything that looks like a combination. He will look for it near the safe, especially in nearby drawers.

HOW BURGLARS OPERATE

The importance of a good, well-hidden safe for valuables is underscored when you know how a typical burglar operates. Once inside a house or apartment (or hotel room) he goes right to the dressing room, if there is one, or to the bureau in the master bedroom. He looks for a jewelry box on the bureau or dressing table. Then he tries the right-hand drawer. Usually he need not go any further.

If there's still no jewelry, he tries each drawer down to the bottom, looking for a locked drawer. A locked one usually means hidden valuables, so he'll jimmy it open. If he gets to the bottom without finding a locked drawer, he opens each drawer on the way up, searching with his hand inside each for a box or bag of jewelry.

If still unsuccessful, he goes to the closet and looks on the shelves. He looks around the closet for a wall safe, and then goes back to the room and looks behind pictures for a wall safe. He'll also try a laundry hamper as well as the bedside table. All this takes him no more than a few minutes. By then, in the average house, he will usually have the jewelry and possibly cash, too, in his pocket. By and large, that's all the professional thief wants. He wants to stir no suspicion by carrying bulky things out of the place. He wants to get out fast and vanish. It's the sneak thief, dope addict, or teen-age burglar who is more likely to pick up everything in sight, such as radios and TV sets, typewriters, fur coats, and jewelry that is easy to find.

WATCHDOGS

A dog will scare off many a potential thief and be a great source of reassurance for the safety of your house and you. It need not be a fierce mastiff. A small terrier can be just as good if he has a watchdog instinct and a big bark. If you want to go all out for your personal safety at home, choose either a trained German shepherd police dog or a Doberman pinscher, the two most popular breeds used for security. A dog specially trained to ward off a potential attacker should not also be counted on to be a friendly playmate and pet, however. In fact, he could be a menace to children and guests.

If you're concerned about reasonably good burglary protection, any good breed with a loud bark and a breed reputation for protecting his master will ordinarily serve as a good watchdog as well as a pet. A German shepherd or Doberman can, of course, also fulfill this role, especially if it has not been trained from birth to be nothing but a police dog.

SPECIAL TIPS

If you do not have a safe, don't put valuables in an obvious place. "Put your mind to it, and you can probably think of a dozen hiding places for your valuables, but don't put them anywhere you think of in the first ten minutes," a top police inspector says. "By that time you will have exhausted the most likely places that everybody thinks of and which any thief worth his salt knows about. After about ten minutes of thinking you've warmed up, and the obvious places are out of your system. Then you're most likely to come up with a really good hiding place." If you're leaving home for a while, take your valuables, including those ordinarily kept in your house safe, to your safe-deposit box.

Don't hire household help in a casual manner, even when it's on a temporary basis, and even though you get the help from an employment agency. An agency may or may not check references, and when it does, it is not always a careful check. Ask for references, and be sure to check them. Verify the home address a potential employee gives you. Does the person really live there? A dishonest employee often gives a false address and stays on the job just long enough to find out what you have that's worth stealing and where it's kept.

Don't leave valuables exposed when workmen and strangers are in and out of the house. Don't put total faith and trust in delivery men and mechanics who visit your house.

The likelihood of retrieving stolen possessions after a burglary is small, according to the police. It's wise, though, to be able to identify your valuables, if only for insurance reasons. You should have a written record of special marks and identification numbers on watches and furs and the serial number of a typewriter, TV set, and other such property. Jewelry and other valuables should be appraised by an expert, who should give you a written technical description of each item appraised. (Insurance for valuables is covered in Chapter 7.)

BURGLARY REVIEW

Put good locks on your doors, which means dead-bolt latches at the very least. Merely locking your doors and windows when you're away is a big step forward in keeping out the run-of-the-mill burglar.

Don't let your house look unoccupied when you're away, and don't announce your absence to one and all. Have neighbors and police keep an eye on your house, and you've taken a major second step forward.

An alarm system can be expensive, but it may be worth the money. One of the best inexpensive alarms is a good dog with a loud and fierce bark.

CHAPTER 10 SELLING A HOUSE FOR THE HIGHEST PRICE

■ *How to get the largest profit when you sell a house . . . Should you use a real-estate broker? . . . Choosing a good broker . . . Giving a broker an "exclusive listing" . . . Selling the house yourself and saving the broker's fee . . . Deciding the sales price for the house . . . Writing a "fact sheet" . . . Preparing the house for sale . . . Advertising and showing the house . . . Negotiating the sale and how to bargain . . . The best time of the year to sell a house . . . Understanding buyer psychology . . . Letting a ·
buyer take over your mortgage or giving your own mortgage to a buyer . . . The income tax due on a profit from selling a house and when a loss is tax deductible.*

THE GOAL is not only to sell your house at a good price but also to sell it fast. The longer a house for sale goes unsold, the lower the price you're likely to get.

How an actual house was sold in record time—a mere five days—not long ago illustrates important things that can make or break the sale. We'll call the couple who sold the house Jack and Mary Lee, not their real names.

They sold their house at a good price and at a profit, but if they had played their cards right, they could have realized about $1,000 to $1,500 more for the house. Their house was a thirty-five-year-old structure of traditional design which they had bought for $19,000 ten years before. They had spent $10,000 on the house for alterations and modernization work. Jack was suddenly transferred to the West Coast, and they had to sell quickly and leave.

Jack was uncertain about how much to sell the house for. To

find out, he hired a real-estate appraiser. The appraiser inspected the house—and the neighborhood—and made a few computations. He estimated that the house was worth $34,500, its current market value.

At the time, late 1969, houses were in increasingly short supply. The Lees' house was located in a desirable suburb, so Jack decided to put the house on the market for $39,500. Mary opposed this. "That's too high," she said. "We'll never sell it."

"Let's try it," Jack said. "I feel we might get it, or close to it. Besides, we can come down in price if necessary," he said.

They advertised the house for three days, starting on a Thursday. Some people called about it by the weekend. Ten different couples made appointments to see the house, and Jack and Mary scheduled them on an hourly basis. There were plenty of buyers around, or so it seemed, and Jack and Mary were encouraged.

On Monday morning one of the people who had seen the house called and made an offer of $37,500 to buy it. Jack and Mary were torn. Though $2,000 below their asking price, that was a good offer, and they had to sell fast, but they wondered about raising the ante to $38,500, say, before they sold.

Suppose that was too much, and the bidder said no? Should they bargain, or just accept the $37,500 price? They were nervous because of the need to sell quickly. Selling fast would be an enormous load off their minds. They called the man back and accepted his offer, selling the house then and there, in five days, for a flat $37,500.

Later that day another man who had seen the house called and offered $36,000 for it. The tone of his voice suggested to Jack that this was an initial bid, and the man was prepared to raise the bid, if necessary. Jack told the man the house had been "sold" earlier, but if the deal fell through, he would call him back.

About a week later the first buyer began hedging. He said he wasn't sure that he could afford $37,500 for the house. Jack and Mary unfortunately did not have anything in writing from the man. They should, of course, have had initial sales papers signed immediately when the verbal offer was accepted,

The Lees were hit by a second stage of nervous apprehension. Suppose the buyer pulled out and they had to sell the house all over again? Time was running out on them. Jack called the stalling buyer and said he would lower the price $500 to $37,000, if the man would sign a sales contract immediately. The man mulled this over and finally said yes. Jack then called a lawyer, who had a contract drawn up, and the sale was consummated in writing.

Reviewing the transaction later, Jack told this author that he had got a good price for the house, but he had also made several mistakes that had cost him as much as $1,500, he figured. First, he should not have come down so fast when the $37,500 offer was first made for the house. He was nervous at the time. He felt now, with hindsight, that he should have responded with an offer to drop his $39,500 price by only $1,000 and that this would have been accepted. Secondly, he should have been prepared to clinch the offer at once in writing. That would have held the buyer to his offered price. Third, he need not have come down that additional $500 later. He felt that the buyer really wanted the house and still would have bought the house without the $500 reduction.

Jack had a big thing going for him. He had a good house to sell at a fair and attractive price. Moreover, houses were in great demand, and many buyers were around. He also had one thing going against him. He and Mary had to sell fast. The urgency of their situation made them apprehensive. It forced them into two financial compromises that cost them as much as $1,500 on the sale of the house. Nonetheless, they still made a profit on the house and, above all, they sold the house fast.

Not everybody manages to sell his house at a profit, though, to be sure, many a person has sold his house at a good profit in recent years. Most of those who bought low and sold high were the beneficiaries of economic happenstance and sometimes sheer luck. Their houses ballooned in value because of inflation. All ships rise when the tide comes in.

At other times, particularly during the Great Depression days of the 1930's and during the late 1950's and early 1960's, many a person sold his house at a loss. The market had softened at those times, as it could very well do again in the future. Even during boom times for housing, people find that they cannot always unload their houses at fancifully high prices. This is especially so for old-fashioned houses, rundown structures, and those located in borderline neighborhoods.

If everything is going for you when you put a house on the market, you'll probably do well, particularly if you know how to sell it properly. At other times, you may not do so well, particularly if you fall prey to certain common mistakes.

SHOULD YOU USE A REAL-ESTATE BROKER?

This can pay for some people and not for others. On the one hand, sell the house yourself, and you stand to save the usual 6 to 7 per cent commission that a broker gets for selling your house. On the other, you might lose more than that if a good broker could have gotten a much higher price for your house than you could have. A good broker can earn his fee by selling the house fast as well as by getting you a higher price. If a broker doesn't sell the house, you owe him nothing (except in rare cases when a special financial arrangement is made).

A broker is especially recommended if you have neither the time nor aptitude nor inclination to sell your own house. A good broker will tell you approximately what your house is worth and how to prepare the house for sale. He will advertise the house at his expense, answer calls about it, handle the negotiations when a hot prospect appears, arrange the sale, and, if necessary, help the buyer get a mortgage to swing the purchase.

You may want to have more than one broker handle the house

on a nonexclusive basis, in which case whoever makes the sale gets the bacon. Though more people are trying to sell your house, this does not necessarily increase the likelihood of a good sale. Each broker listing the house will bring around prospects he has who want to buy a house, but that's about all many will do.

Knowing that other brokers are on the house, too, the usual broker is less motivated to devote additional time and effort to selling your house. This, however, depends on the house, each broker's assessment of his chance of selling it, and the size of the commission he'll earn: in other words, the price of the house. You can also try to sell your house at the same time yourself. If you deal with the final buyer without benefit of a broker, you do not pay any broker.

The exception is when you have an exclusive agreement with a single broker to sell your house. You give him and him alone the right to list and sell your house. No other broker may handle the house unless it's through the first broker. The agreement usually extends for ninety days, after which time you may renew the agreement or drop it. An exclusive listing gives a broker special incentive to sell your house, and he will generally invest more time and money in the effort. An exclusive agreement also *may* require that the broker get a sales commission, even if you yourself sell the house cold to an unexpected buyer. This depends on your written agreement with the broker.

An exclusive agreement with one broker is particularly recommended if you must move away before your house is sold. Given an exclusive, a good broker will not only try harder to sell the house, but he can watch the house and handle various matters for you when you're far away.

Choosing a Broker

If you use a broker, especially on an exclusive basis, it's important to choose a good one. There are over half a million licensed real-estate agents and brokers in the country, but more than half are part-time agents who are cab drivers, housewives, and insurance salesmen or are otherwise employed or unemployed. The best brokers are usually those who are in the real-estate business full time. They are the ones who devote the most time to each house they handle.

By and large, the best brokers are "realtors," licensed real-estate brokers who are also members of the local Real Estate Board and of the National Association of Real Estate Boards. There are only about eighty thousand realtors all told in the United States. A realtor is bound by a code of ethics designed to maintain honest dealings with the public. An action that violates the code can cause him to be tossed out of the local real-estate board and perhaps even lose his license to sell houses.

A realtor can also offer other advantages. For example, you sometimes get the benefit of a multiple listing of your house, even though you list it with only one realtor. Your house is given out by your realtor to other realtor members in the area. You get greater marketing coverage. If, as a result, another realtor lands a buyer, he splits the fee with your realtor. This also can be done when you give a realtor an exclusive listing. In other words, an exclusive listing with a single realtor does not necessarily restrict the house to sale by merely one realtor. The multiple listing service provides more widespread sales exposure, though your realtor remains the primary broker.

A realtor can be identified by the word itself on a real-estate broker's card and place of business. Sometimes it's mentioned with his name in the classified telephone pages under "Real Estate." To be sure, ask a broker if he is a realtor. If he is not, he still may be a perfectly good broker; in general, however, a realtor is a better choice than a nonrealtor agent.

SAVING THE BROKER'S SALES FEE

You can save that 6 or 7 per cent commission (more for a farm or rural house) if you sell your house yourself. That assumes, however, that you can sell it just as well as a broker and get as high a price for the house as a broker would get for you.

The easiest time to sell a house is obviously during a seller's market. That's especially during a housing shortage when more people seek houses than there are houses for sale. During the height of the housing shortage of the late 1960's one prominent real-estate broker in a New York suburb said he could sell ten houses for every house he could get to list. Throngs of buyers were looking for houses, but very few good houses were available for sale. You might wonder why you should give an agent your house to sell at such a time. It would seem that you could merely put an ad in the paper and be swamped with inquiries. It's not quite that easy—but if you decide to sell a house without an agent, here is how to do it successfully.

Price the House Right

Overpricing is by far the biggest single mistake made when amateurs sell their own houses. It's often the result of a wild dream of making a lot of money. The dream is punctured after person after person says, "No thank you, the price is too high."

Take, for example, a man who put a modest three-bedroom house on the market not long ago for $45,000. Some ten to fifteen years previously the house had been worth about $17,500, but other houses nearby had recently sold for $40,000 to $45,000 as a result of inflation and because the small suburban village in which it was located was a nice place to live. Nonetheless, the house has gone unsold for more than two years, as this is being written.

After two years the man dropped his price to $40,000, but he told the author of this book, "I'll accept a little less if I get a good enough offer." The house has not sold because it lacks modern features like a new kitchen and bathroom that other similar houses had that did sell for up to $45,000. And it is not a very large house. In short, the house was not worth $40,000 to $45,000 even in a seller's market.*

An overpriced house that goes unsold tends to develop a stigma as it stands, apparently unwanted. Word spreads that something is wrong. Almost invariably, the owner must later reduce his

---

* Just before this book went to press the man had dropped his price to $35,000, but the house was still unsold.

price, often quite sharply. He generally could have obtained a higher price at the beginning if the house was priced right. In addition, if you sell a house quickly, you avoid paying additional taxes and insurance on it. The owner of the house just mentioned has, at this writing, paid some two thousand dollars in taxes and insurance on his unsold, unoccupied house, not to mention the loss on the capital invested in the house while it goes unsold.

Pricing is an important and delicate decision. The best advice: Hire a good real-estate appraiser to tell you the current market value of the house. A good appraiser will inspect the house and the neighborhood. He should also know, or find out, what other comparable houses have recently sold for in your neighborhood. Then he'll give you his professional estimate of the house value. This figure is based on such things as the size and condition of the house and value of your lot, mixed with a stirring of "feel" for the real-estate market. The appraiser's charge ordinarily will range from about $25 for a low-priced house up to $75 to $100, depending on the house and where you live. It is worth it. The names of local appraisers should be obtainable from a local bank or from the classified pages of the telephone book.

You could also ask a few real-estate brokers what your house is worth, but you may or may not get good free advice. One trap to avoid is a real-estate broker who goes overboard on his suggested price deliberately. This breed will mention a fancifully high figure with the purpose of getting you to list your house only with him. Once he's got your house to sell, he makes a limited effort and then returns and says, "I'm sorry, but I'm afraid you must lower the price. The market's soft. Nobody is interested unless you lower the price." You either lower the price and he sells it—at about the same, lower price that other agents originally mentioned—or you don't lower it, and you probably never hear from him again.

The price a good appraiser or broker mentions will usually be approximately what you should get for the house. Then you can put the house up for sale at about 10 to 15 per cent higher. This gives you a cushion for bargaining, allowing you to come down in price when a hot prospect makes a lower offer.

Say, for example, your house is realistically worth $35,000. That's close to the top price you should get for the house. You then put the house on the market for $37,500 to $38,500 or perhaps go up 15 per cent to $40,250. In this last case, however, use prudence. Price it at $39,950, since going over $40,000 has the psychological impact of making the price seem $10,000 higher.

Don't put the price too high if you must sell the house fast. Raise it a small percentage, no more than 5 to 10 per cent. If you have all the time in the world, raise it somewhat higher. Again, this takes a feel for the market and a willingness to wait longer to sell.

Bargaining for houses is accepted practice in most areas. There may be less bargaining during a housing shortage, where the seller is in the driver's seat, assuming that you've got a good house for sale. Then you can hold fairly firmly to your price or reduce it a bit to give a potential buyer the feeling that you're giving him a break so that he will buy then and there. During a buyer's market, on the other hand, you may have to drop the price quite a bit to sell, again depending largely on the house and its desirability, coupled with how much a buyer wants the house.

Bargaining is sometimes not customary; the price is "firm." You may specifically say this, setting the price exactly at the figure you want and making it clear that that's it. If a man is interested in buying, he must pay that price. If not, he says, "No, thank you," and he disappears from the scene. Generally, the price on a house is assumed to be negotiable. The seller tacitly announces that, if necessary, he's willing to lower the price to sell. He may indicate this in an ad, for instance, by saying "asking price." A buyer gets the message. The seller means business and will come down if necessary to sell the house. All of that must be considered and weighed by you to determine the price you put on your house.

Prepare a "Fact Sheet" about the House

A fact sheet is a typed sheet or two giving vital statistics about the house. It should include such things as the size of the house in terms of number of rooms and square feet of living area, size of the lot, annual taxes, heating bills, and the location of nearby schools, shopping centers, and churches.

Also note special features—especially those that may not be obvious. This may mean copper plumbing; insulation; special-quality fixtures in the kitchen, bathroom, or anywhere else; and any feature that is beyond the ordinary and not found in most houses. If you have installed new equipment or remodeled within recent years, say so in the fact sheet. That means a new furnace, central air-conditioning, new wiring, a water heater, a new roof, and so on.

Don't go overboard on the fact sheet. Present the facts as they are, and leave out the adjectives. (Remember Flaubert's "The adjective is the enemy of the verb." It's also the enemy of the noun.) Inform, don't inflate. The more informative the fact sheet and the less it sounds like an overblown commercial, the more effective it will be.

Your fact sheet can be especially effective if you also include minor drawbacks or flaws, even a major flaw, particularly if it is an obvious one. Say that the basement has a damp spot on the wall or some windows do not open. This can gain the confidence of a potential buyer. The house may need some rewiring or a new water-heater—say so, but make an allowance for repairing the defect by lowering your asking price for the house accordingly. That could mean an allowance of $400 to $500 for the cost of the new wiring or $150 to $175 for the cost of the new water-heater. At worst, you may have to reduce your asking price by that much to sell, a small price to pay for a quick sale.

Advertise Effectively

If you're selling your house yourself, put a carefully written ad in the best local paper for real-estate advertising. That's the paper with the largest classified real-estate section. Consider using a large metropolitan paper, even if you live in a suburb with local papers, especially if many commuters live in your area. Still another commuter may wish to move out.

The weekend is usually the best time to advertise. Most papers publish their large real-estate section on Saturday or Sunday; sometimes it's Friday. Definitely advertise on that particular day.

Tell friends, relatives, and neighbors that the house is for sale. Take advantage of free advertising. Put a free ad in the company newspaper published where you work, or put a notice on the bulletin board. Call the personnel manager of any large national company, such as General Electric, I.B.M., or General Motors, that has a major office nearby. They continually transfer employees and often seek news about houses their people could buy.

Prepare the House for Sale

Before people are due to arrive, be sure the house is ready. Put your best foot forward. Tidy up, of course, but also mend and spruce up. There's no need to redecorate and paint the inside; in fact, spending money for redecoration to sell a house is inadvisable and usually a waste of money. Nearly every buyer has his own ideas about redecorating.

Do, however, consider repainting the exterior if it's necessary. As mentioned earlier in this book, this is one of the few major expenses advisable to sell a house. It can substantially increase the appeal of a house and you may sometimes recover more than the price of the painting. Patch up elsewhere with paint. Fill in cracks in walks, driveway, and walls. Fix a broken step. Don't overlook a leaky faucet, and perhaps most important of all, make the entrance to the house look good. If, for example, the front doorknob comes off in the hand of an entering prospect, it can leave a lasting impression on the black side. He'll imagine that the whole house is loaded with flaws, mostly invisible, and a no-sale bell rings in his mind. Don't forget to clean up the cellar and the attic. These chores take a little time, effort, and perhaps a little repair money to a serviceman, but they're essential to give people a good first—and last—impression of your house.

If you must move out before the house is sold, try to leave some furnishings in it. Brokers say it is ten times harder to sell an empty house than it is to sell a furnished house. Furniture gives a house a lived-in look. So if you move, forestall that big old empty look by leaving the house partly furnished if at all possible.

Showing the House

Show it by appointment only. Get the name, address, and phone number of each person who calls and shows interest. Some inevitably will forget to show up or will blithely break their appointment. If you have a phone number, obtained when a person first called, you can phone and find out if he is really coming.

When a prospect is scheduled to visit, get children, pets, and visiting in-laws out of the house or secluded in a distant room. When the prospect arrives, have him sit for a moment and discreetly feel him out. Real-estate brokers call this qualifying the prospect. Is he really an interested buyer, or is he just a looker? Let him read your fact sheet, but get this sheet back from him. If a person wants to keep it, just say, "No, it's confidential information that the person who buys the house may not want other people to have." The eventual buyer will appreciate this.

Lead people informally through the house. Let them do the talking, and listen for significant comments. You'll be surprised what people like and do not like about homes. Don't be obtrusive, and don't talk the prospects' ears off. Let your house speak for itself.

You can, however, quietly point out special features that might be overlooked, such as Thermopane glass in the windows, extra storage built in to the house, a special point about the floor plan or room arrangement, outdoor lights, and so on. Don't overdo it. Watching a good real-estate broker take people through a house can be a revealing lesson. A good broker uses the soft sell. He doesn't high-pressure prospects. One prominent broker says, "People buying a house want to make up their own minds. They want to take their time doing it, too. Putting pressure on them makes them feel forced into something they don't want. It often backfires."

Some people go through the house like the wind and are gone

forever. They probably never intended to buy, or if they did, they want a sixty-thousand-dollar house for thirty thousand dollars. One who is truly interested will slow down, go around a second time, poking into closets and out-of-the-way places. He might not say much, but his actions speak louder. He will ask questions and then probably say he'll be in touch with you. Don't necessarily believe all who say that, but a few will call back in a day or two and ask more questions or ask to see the house again. One might make you an offer.

Negotiating the Sale

This is an art. It sometimes takes nerves of steel. Assume you get an offer for your house. You may even be offered the full price you're asking. Be prepared to clinch the deal immediately. You should have the necessary papers on hand and ready to be signed. This may require lining up a lawyer early. A good real-estate broker who is handling things for you will also know how to clinch the deal. In some areas it is customary for a buyer to sign a "binder" or "offer-to-purchase" agreement, though it may be called something else. In others a conditional sales contract is signed, and the buyer gives a deposit. The deposit is returnable, however, if the buyer cannot obtain a mortgage to buy the house. Sometimes the sale is also contingent on structural inspection of the house. Whatever the customs and legalities where you live, you should know about them in advance. Then you play the game by feel and intuition.

The tighter the supply of houses, the more likely it is that someone will pay the price you ask, or nearly so, and a quick sale follows. If you receive an offer or two lower than your asking price, serious negotiations must follow. Some people don't mean business but nonetheless will make a ridiculously low offer. They have no intention of paying more. Chalk them off unless you have no other buyer and are forced to sell.

Ordinarily a person will bid about 10 to 20 per cent lower than your asking price. He does this deliberately, figuring that you'll come down a little and he'll come up a little. You return the ball, saying perhaps that you'll come down a little, and then wait a few days for his response. If he raises his offer, you're probably on your way. You can probably sell the house at a price about halfway between your initial asking price and his initial bid. If you need not sell in a hurry and want more money, then you merely drop your price a little to the lowest figure you'll accept, and that's that. The man can take it or leave it.

Don't be too rigid, however. As a rule, it's best to accept the first really good offer made for a house after it's put on the market. There's an initial stir and interest in a house at that time, but after a period of several weeks the interest subsides. Turn down a near-acceptable offer, and you may find yourself in the midst of a long dry spell of no interest in your house and no sale.

The time of the year can be a factor in selling the house. Most houses are bought and sold in the spring and early summer of each year, from about April 15 to July 4. Sales slow down in summer, when people go on vacation, and then speed up again in September until about the middle of October. Many are reluctant to move after that because school has started, and they don't want to move their children to another school. Sales slow down to virtually nothing as Christmas approaches and then start up slowly again in January.

Understanding the Home Buyer

Here is how one couple bought a house at a time when there was a rather even balance between supply and demand. Jack Briggs and his wife had been shopping for a house for several months when they found the one they wanted. It was an older house owned by a man named Wilson, for sale at $38,500. Jack doubted that it was worth that much, so he hired a real-estate appraiser to appraise it. The man figured that the house was worth $35,850, its current market value. He charged Jack a fee of $45.

Jack was a thorough guy. He called a professional engineer to inspect the house and check its structural condition. This cost $55, but it was worth it in terms of insurance. The engineer cited a few flaws but found nothing alarming. A new furnace might be needed in a few years, and the house was not insulated. Some rewiring would be needed, and the foundation needed a little shoring up in one place. The house would also need a paint job, and Jack's wife figured on some kitchen modernization, though not a whole new kitchen. In all, Jack calculated that about $2,000 to $3,000 would be required ultimately for repairs and improvements.

The house was overpriced, but how much could he buy it for? Armed with known facts about the house, Jack and his wife decided they would pay $35,500 or $36,000, their absolute limit. Jack told his wife he would offer Wilson $33,500 for the house as his first bid.

His wife nearly screamed with alarm. She said Mr. Wilson would be insulted. "He won't speak to us any more!"

"Hold on," Jack said. "He'll probably turn it down, but we've got to start low to leave room for negotiations." She continued to object, and Jack finally said reluctantly that he'd make it $34,000, but not a penny more, on the first go-around.

Jack called Wilson and said he liked the house. Exaggerating a little, he said it needed about $3,000 to $4,000 worth of improvements, painting, insulation, and so on. Therefore Jack simply could not pay $38,500, the asking price. Jack took a deep breath and told Wilson he would give him $34,000 for the house.

Wilson laughed. "I'm sorry," he said, "you'll have to do better than that."

Jack said, "Think it over and let me know. If you can come down, give us a call." They left it at that.

Jack waited a few days, and sure enough Wilson called back. He told Jack, "Look, I'd like to sell the house fast. If you want to do business now, you can have it for thirty-seven five, a thousand dollars off the price. Another family is interested, and a broker is bringing them over this afternoon. I like you and your wife, so

I thought I'd call you back and let you know. Thirty-seven five, that's the best I can do."

Jack said he'd talk to his wife and call back.

Jack's wife began to panic. "We'll never get the house now," she said, "Especially if somebody else is seeing it."

"Don't worry," Jack said. "There's always somebody else in the wings. That's what they always say."

Jack was concerned too, though. Suppose there was another buyer who offered more? Jack told his wife, "I'll call him back in the morning. Besides, I've got an idea. Two can play the game. I'll just tell him that we're considering another house." He added, "Luckily we're dealing direct with him. He won't pay a broker's commission selling to us. If there's really another guy in the picture with a broker, it's going to cost Wilson six per cent."

Jack did some figuring on a piece of paper and said, "If the other guy pays the full price, thirty-eight five, the broker gets his cut, and Wilson ends up with thirty-six thousand, one hundred and ninety dollars net for the house.

His wife said, "That's still more than our offer. We have to meet that."

"No," Jack said. "Chances are the other guy will offer less. Wilson probably won't get more than thirty-six thousand. Maybe a little more, maybe less."

Jack called Wilson back the next day and said he and his wife would like another look at the home. Jack really wanted to make his next offer face to face with Wilson rather than on the phone.

At the house Jack and his wife checked a few things and then sat down with Wilson. Jack braced himself as he prepared to make another offer. He said finally, "We still like the house, but the best we can offer is thirty-five five." He waited a moment and added his kicker. "We've been looking at another house we like a lot too. I thought we'd come over here once more and give our final offer. I would like to make it higher," he said, "but I simply can't."

Wilson said, "I'm afraid that's not enough. I've already come down a thousand dollars. I'm just not prepared to sell for less." He proceeded to recount all the special features of the house and the things he had done to improve it. He all but said that Jack's offer was unthinkable, but they parted amicably.

Wilson had deliberately feigned unconcern. After Jack and his wife left, he began wondering if he would ever sell the house. The people whom the broker had brought over had turned out to be duds. The man had offered a mere $35,000 flat—that was all. Of all the nerve, Wilson thought. And the broker would get 6 per cent of that. Well, maybe he could come down to $37,000, and Briggs would buy. Who knows?

If not, however, he might not sell the house for months. The market was getting tougher, and there weren't many buyers. Was Briggs kidding about buying another house? He would wait a few days, and maybe Briggs would call. Or maybe he should phone and come down another five hundred—maybe even a thousand. He would delay a little more, but he did not want to hold off too long. He might see his only prospect take off and buy another house.

Jack and his wife were also suffering nerve pangs. They are par for the course during such negotiations, he reminded himself. You need a stout heart and a firm hold on your nerves. Fortunately, they were not compelled to leave their present house and they could take their time. Jack thought that if he held off a few days longer, he might save another five hundred or thousand dollars. He would pay up to $36,000 for the house, but no more.

Things stood that way for several days. Both men fought the temptation to call the other. Wilson called the broker to see if any other prospective buyer had showed up, but the broker said no. If Wilson came down in price, the broker said he might be able to stir up new interest, but as of now, he had exhausted every prospect for the house.

Wilson called Jack the next day. He could not hold back any longer. He said, "My wife wants to sell right away, and maybe we still can get together." If Jack really wanted the house, Wilson said, he could have it for thirty-six five. "How's that?" Wilson asked.

Jack avoided a direct answer. They talked for a while, each feeling out the other. Jack's wife, standing at his elbow, urged him to accept Wilson's offer. Jack shook his head and continued on the phone with Wilson. "I just don't know what to do," Jack said.

A pause. Then Jack said, "Make it thirty-six even, and it's a deal."

Another pause. Wilson said, "Okay, you've got yourself a house. I'll take it."

The house was sold to Jack for $36,000, or about 10 per cent below the original asking price.

Remember that Jack bought Wilson's house at a time when there was roughly an even balance in the supply and demand for houses. During a buyer's market Jack could have bought the house for less. Wilson probably would have had to reduce his price more to sell. Conversely, during a seller's market Jack probably would have had to pay more. Other buyers would very likely have competed with him for the house, and Wilson could have held steady for a higher price.

Scout the market before selling a house. Talk to your bank (the people who have your present mortgage) as well as to brokers and others in the business. This will help you determine how high to price your house and how much negotiating may be necessary when a buyer appears.

Talk to brokers and a few bankers about the mortgage terms that are available to buy your house. Knowing the kind of mortgage terms, including cash down-payment required, will help you qualify buyers. If, for example, eight thousand dollars in cash will be required to buy your house, you won't want to waste time on prospects without that kind of money. You could lower your price, thus lowering the down payment required, but then you will lose money. You'll have all the figures at your fingertips if you've talked to a few banks about financing the house.

Should you let a buyer take over your mortgage? In a tight mortgage market this may be the only way a buyer can finance the house and you can sell it. It can also be a good thing for both the buyer and you at any time if your mortgage is fairly large, compared with the new mortgages available from banks.

You might also consider giving your own mortgage to a buyer, another out when mortgages are high in price and hard to come by. During the tight mortgage period starting in 1969, this was the only way some people could sell their houses. To do it, the seller simply performs like a bank. He gets a down payment from the buyer and gives the buyer a mortgage loan with the same terms as a bank. The buyer agrees to pay him back monthly for X number of years and at Y interest rate.

A lawyer is mandatory for your own protection when you either let a buyer take over your mortgage or when you give him the mortgage. There are pitfalls to avoid, and only a good lawyer can help you avoid them. He will write the formal contract and loan papers. This advice cannot be overemphasized, especially since the legalities involved vary from state to state. The legal language required to protect you against any eventuality will be known only by a lawyer familiar with the law in your state.

INCOME-TAX REVIEW

If you make money on the sale of your house, the profit is taxable, as explained in Chapter 1. To review the tax rules: If you use the money you received from the sale to buy another house within twelve months or build a new house within eighteen months, the tax is deferred. It is not canceled. If you buy and sell a series of houses, the tax on the profit from each sale is deferred until you sell a house at no profit or at a loss or until you sell your last house. Then you're liable for a tax on the total accumulated profit from each sale, going back to the first house you bought and sold. That future tax bill can be kept to a minimum by keeping records of every expense for capital improvements on each house. Also keep a record of the expenses you incurred in buying each house, such as closing costs, title insurance, and other such fees, and expenses incurred when you sell the house. Capital improvements add to your basic cost of the house and therefore mean less net profit on the sale. This situation is also discussed in Chapter 1.

You ordinarily get no tax benefit if you sell a house at a loss unless you have rented out the house for at least six months before selling it. Then the loss is a business loss and is tax deductible. To qualify for that loss, you must prove to the Internal Revenue Service that you rented the house in good faith. If you're likely to sell a house at a loss, it could be a good idea to consult a good tax man for advice, especially if a lot of money is at stake.

SUMMARY

A fast sale at a high price depends very much on pricing the house properly and not overpricing it. The house should look its best. Prospects are snagged by a good advertisement, especially a weekend ad in the newpaper that most people buy for real-estate ads.

The legal requirements for a sale can be crucial, which is where a good lawyer can help you; you'll generally need a lawyer for the closing, so you might as well hire him early.

Homeowner's Checklist

HERE IS a checklist review of the main points of this book. It will give you a quick reminder of important information.

CHAPTER 1: TAXES AND MORTGAGES

- Your house assessment: Verify it and check how it was determined by the tax assessor. Is it based on the accurate market value for your house? On accurate cost data (such as the price you paid for the house)? It also should be proportionate to the assessments of other houses nearby, especially those of comparable size, type, and value.
- Should your assessment be reduced? If it's more than a little high, discuss it with the tax assessor. If necessary, discuss it with a local lawyer, and determine the customary local procedure for appealing it. Go ahead and appeal only if you can establish a strong case for a reduction.
- Do you qualify for a tax exemption? Determine what real-estate exemptions are given locally (such as veterans' or homestead or those given to homeowners age sixty-five and over). You generally apply for one on a form available at the tax assessor's office.
- Household-property tax: Don't take it for granted. Review it periodically, and be sure you're not paying too much.
- Income-tax savings: Do you take the full allowable deduction on your house-mortgage interest, property taxes, and possible other house expenses on your income-tax return each year? You should also maintain a running record of all house expenses for when you may sell your house at a profit and then owe a capital-gains tax on the sale.
- Mortgage payments: Don't pay off your mortgage ahead of

225

time unless it really pays. This depends on the mortgage interest you pay balanced against the return you would get on the same money invested elsewhere.

▪ Business use of house: If your house is used in part for business, be sure to get the proper tax deduction for it.

CHAPTER 2: UTILITY BILLS

▪ Gas versus electricity: Determine which is cheaper for appliances in your area. Then the kitchen range, water heater, and clothes dryer in particular should all be on the cheaper one. Remember this when you buy replacement appliances.

▪ Know the appliances that use a lot of electricity, as noted on pages 24–25, and use them efficiently.

▪ Know how your gas and electric bills work and how to check them.

▪ Avoid common mistakes that often waste gas and electricity, particularly in the kitchen.

▪ Use low-wattage or fluorescent bulbs for lights left on for long periods, but don't sacrifice good illumination for questionable economy.

▪ Chart your gas and electric bills, and check them once or twice a year.

▪ Periodically inspect for common water leaks, and eliminate them.

CHAPTER 3: TELEPHONE BILLS

▪ Get credit for wrong numbers, disconnects, and cutoffs (merely by notifying the operator).

▪ Review your monthly billing plan every year or so. You might do better to change to another plan. Investigate special auxiliary billing plans that might save you money.

▪ Know which local calls can be made at no charge and which cost you extra.

▪ Be familiar with the long-distance charges within your state and for out-of-state calls. Make a personal table of the time periods when you can save money on long-distance calls you frequently make.

▪ In general, call station-to-station rather than person-to-person.

▪ Eliminate special telephone equipment or accessories that are unnecessary or not worth the extra monthly rental charge.

▪ Don't call long distance indiscriminately from a toll phone or hotel room, collect, or with a credit card. The charge for each can be considerably more than the same call dialed from a home or office telephone.

CHAPTER 4: HOME-REPAIR BILLS

▪ Before calling a serviceman when a breakdown occurs, check first that the electricity is on and the controls are properly set, and look for a possible problem that you can solve yourself.

▪ Know the kind of preventive maintenance that will prolong the life of different appliances. Read the manufacturer's instructions.

▪ Establish a good relationship with a few reliable appliance dealers and repairmen. Buy your household equipment and appliances from those you can count on for good service and who, over the years, will take care of you.

▪ Home maintenance: Set up a periodic maintenance schedule for those parts of the house most susceptible to trouble and break-downs—roof gutters, outside water drainage, plumbing drains, door and window caulking, termite and wood-rot areas, etc.

CHAPTER 5: HEATING

▪ Insulate, weather-strip, and, depending on your climate, put up storm doors and storm windows. These reduce heat leakage from your house and also prevent house walls and other surfaces from getting excessively chilled. Use the palm test to determine where heat may be leaking excessively from your house.

▪ Be sure your heating plant is operating efficiently. Have a CO_2 test done, especially with oil heat. An oil burner should also be cleaned and adjusted at least once a year.

▪ What is the cheapest fuel for heating in your area? Have you determined this with certainty (not just taken someone's casual word)? If you do not use that fuel, naturally you should consider the cost of switching to it for future savings.

▪ Find and cultivate a really good heating serviceman. Deal honestly with him, and he should reciprocate with reliable service. If you have central air-conditioning, use a man who specializes in both heating and cooling.

▪ Forced warm-air heat should have its air filter cleaned regularly, as needed, and it will operate best on the "Continuous Air Circulation" principle; i.e., continuous blower operation.

▪ With hot-water and steam heat, be sure that the air can flow freely under and around radiators. Bleed the radiator valves periodically, and put aluminum foil behind the radiators.

▪ Electric heat demands thick quantities of insulation in walls and ceiling. Storm doors and windows are also required except possibly in the warm South or if you have double-pane window glass like Thermopane or Twindow.

▪ Turn your thermostat down five or six degrees at night to save fuel only if your house is insulated and when the outdoor temperature is no colder than 0° F.

CHAPTER 6: AIR CONDITIONING

▪ Cut heat entry to your house: Shade windows from hot sun, use plenty of thermal insulation (particularly at the attic floor), and ventilate the attic with an adequate fan.

▪ Eliminate common causes of excessive heat and humidity such as excess kitchen heat, an unvented clothes-dryer, a wet cellar, and fabric shower-curtains.

• Operate the air-conditioner efficiently. Keep the air filters clean, set the blower for continuous operation, don't change the thermostat setting all the time, and especially during a heat wave take advantage of twenty-four-hour storage effect by setting the thermostat down a few degrees at night.

• A room air-conditioner, like a central system, will also benefit by a reduction in the house heat-load. And, of course, keep the filter clean, and operate the equipment efficiently. That's the same general advice, but the details are somewhat different for a room cooler.

• Buying new air-conditioning requires that you shop for and choose a really good dealer. This is the number one prerequisite for a good system.

CHAPTER 7: INSURANCE

• Don't be underinsured because of inflation. Periodically check that your house insurance is adequate. Your house insurance should equal at least 80 per cent of the present-day replacement (rebuilding) cost of your house less the value of your land. Also be sure that your personal-property and liability coverage are adequate.

• Do you have a homeowners policy? Is it the best kind for you? If you do not have a homeowners policy, you should determine whether or not it will give you better insurance coverage than what you have now and possibly at less cost than you pay now.

• Take advantage of all available deductible options with your policy. Changing a policy to include deductibles (or making any other changes) can be made at any time; you need not wait until the renewal date.

• Valuable personal property should be adequately insured (unless you don't want to be reimbursed in full in case of loss). You may need a Personal Articles Floater to insure your valuable possessions, and it can pay to investigate this.

- Are you dealing with a good agent and a reliable company? How often has your agent suggested a checkup of your coverage? Has he helped you determine the up-to-date replacement cost of your house? Is the company licensed to sell insurance in your state? Have other people you know fared well on claims with the company?

- Do you have photographs of your house, inside and out? Of your personal property, including furnishings? Keep these in a safe-deposit box, your office, or other safe place away from home.

- Know what to do promptly after a fire or accident or any loss, and know what is covered by your insurance. (Both are given in the policy.)

CHAPTER 8: HOME IMPROVEMENTS AND REMODELING

- Before launching a home-improvement or remodeling project, rethink the job. Is it truly wanted and needed? Is it suitable for your house? Will it really improve your house and increase both the livability and value of the house, or can you do better in another way?

- For a large or important job, consider hiring an architect for advice or complete plans. A good architect will be well worth his fee, whether it's for a few hours' consultation or complete plans.

- Obtain at least two to three bids from different contractors. Be sure each man is bidding on the same work.

- Before choosing a contractor, check on the man. Is he well established locally? Get a credit check (through your bank), check his references (his bank), and call a few people he has done work for.

- Before signing a contract, be sure the contract clearly specifies the work to be done, special features you want, and the type and grade of materials and products to be used, as well as the price.

- Should you be your own contractor? You might save 10 to 20 percent of the total price, but it will require much of your time, effort, and supervision. It's recommended chiefly for a small job that involves no more than three or four subcontractors. In most cases, it's best to hire one contractor to do the whole job.

▪ If you finance the work, compare the cost of refinancing your house mortgage to pay for the job with the cost of an F.H.A. or other home-improvement loan. Shop for a loan, and compare the total cost of credit charged by each potential lender with that charged by others.

▪ While the work is being done, stay out of the workmen's way, but do watch that it is done properly. If you desire a change or additional work, put it in writing along with the additional price to be charged.

CHAPTER 9: THEFT AND BURGLARY

▪ Do you have good, reliable locks on your house doors?
▪ Are vulnerable windows reasonably safe from easy entry?
▪ When you are leaving home: Notify the police that you'll be away; arrange for newspapers, mail, and other deliveries to be stopped; have grass trimmed and, if necessary, snow shoveled from your sidewalks; and install a timer or two that will automatically turn on a few lights in the evening, turning them off later.

▪ Valuable possessions should be kept in a good safe or special locked closet. Valuable papers, precious jewelry, heirlooms, and so on should be kept in a safe-deposit box (unless, of course, you use them frequently). You could also consider a good alarm system for your house.

▪ Get a good watchdog. A good dog, properly loved and cared for, can add much pleasure and joy to life as well as reward you by protecting you against a housebreaker.

CHAPTER 10: SELLING A HOUSE

▪ Should you use a real-estate broker? Definitely yes, if you're disinclined or personally unequipped to advertise, merchandise, show your house, and negotiate the sale. Also, if you must move quickly to a distant city, leave the house in the hands of a good broker. Sell the house yourself and save the broker's fee only if you definitely feel you can handle the total sales effort and have the time and inclination to do it well by yourself.

▪ What sales price should be put on the house? The best way to determine this is by hiring a good real-estate appraiser for a professional estimate of the market value of the house. Increase the asking price a bit according to current market conditions. Talk to brokers, too, and try to determine what comparable houses nearby have sold for recently. Do not, however, overprice the house—this could be a grievous error.

▪ Write a fact sheet describing the house. Put down the facts in a straightforward manner, and don't exaggerate. Exaggeration and overstatement breed suspicion.

▪ Prepare the house properly. Clean up, paint if necessary, and put your best foot forward. Remember that much money could be at stake; there's a big difference between what people will pay for attractive merchandise and the lesser value put on an unattractive product.

▪ Advertise and show the house by appointment only. Merchandise it like a professional (or else let a good broker do it for you). Understand buyer-seller psychology in real estate, and perform accordingly.

▪ If necessary, bargain discreetly, and be prepared to negotiate for the best possible price. You may have to come down in price or otherwise not be able to sell the place.

▪ Consult a lawyer early in the game, and be ready to consummate the sale quickly and legally. Also know the best way a buyer can get a mortgage and finance the purchase, including whether or not letting him take over your mortgage would be a good thing.

INDEX